KNOWING THE FATHER

T H E

JESUS IS THE WAY

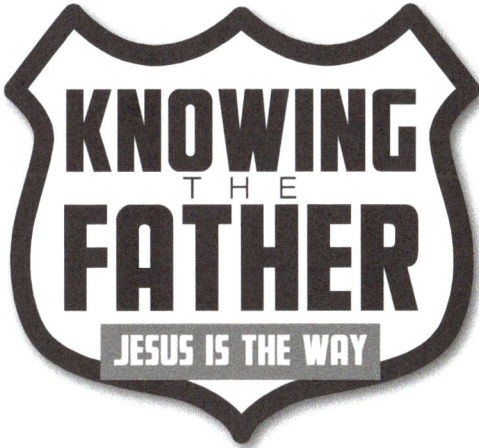

Prison Alliance

Write us a letter and enroll
in our Bible Study today!
PO Box 97095, Raleigh, NC 27624

KNOWING THE FATHER
JESUS IS THE WAY

Stephen E. Canup

Special thanks to Rev. Don Castleberry, Founder
Freedom in Jesus Prison Ministries

Published by:
Freedom in Jesus Prison Ministries
www.fijm.org | info@fijm.org

ACKNOWLEDGEMENTS

Everyone needs a mature spiritual mentor and trusted account-ability partner. I love and appreciate Don Castleberry for fulfilling this role for me. His trust, time and commitment to me have been invaluable. He has become one of my very best friends.

Rev. Don Castleberry is the Founder of Freedom in Jesus Prison Ministries. Learn more about this anointed prison ministry at www.fijm.org or, write to Freedom in Jesus Prison Ministries, P.O. Box 939, Levelland, TX 79336. You may e-mail us at info@fijm.org

Special thanks to Kevin Williamson for cover creation, layout and design assistance. For inquiries about his work, contact Kevin at kevin@kevinwilliamsondesign.com

Appreciation is also expressed for printing and shipping services through Perfection Press. For information contact Robert Riggs, rriggs@printedtoperfection.com

TABLE OF CONTENTS

PREFACE

In the real and currently raging Battle of the Ages between Good and evil, Light and darkness, God and devil-being fought in the Spiritual realm but manifesting in the physical-the enemy has been working to totally destroy the family unit.

God's plan has always been one man married to one woman living and raising children together in a loving, safe, supportive environment; and, instilling in their children Godly morals and ethics. Increasingly too many families are failing.

According to a report entitled "The Father Absence Crisis in America" from the National Fatherhood Initiative, *Father Facts, Eighth Edition*, 18.4 million children (1 in 4) are living without a biological, step, or adoptive father at home.

Research shows when a child is raised in a father-absent home, they are affected in the following ways:

- 4 times greater risk of poverty
- More likely to have behavioral problems
- 2 times greater risk of infant mortality
- More likely to go to prison
- More likely to commit crime
- 7 times more likely to become pregnant as a teen
- More likely to face abuse and neglect
- More likely to abuse drugs and alcohol
- 2 times more likely to suffer obesity
- 2 times more likely to drop out of school

There has never been a more important time to understand, appreciate and receive the goodness, love, mercy, care, and concern of our Heavenly Father for His children. Even among those already in the body of Christ, there are many spiritual orphans.

God longs to be Father to the fatherless. He always loves. He never rejects, shuns, abandons, or abuses His children.

"For I know the plans I have for you," declares the Lord, "plans to prosper you and not to harm you, plans to give you hope and a future. Then you will call on me and come and pray to me, and I will listen to you. You will seek me and find me when you seek me with all your heart." Jeremiah 29:11-13

If you've ever been unloved, rejected, hurt, abused, abandoned, ridiculed, or shamed, you will find healing and acceptance in the Arms of your Heavenly Father. I pray the information and revelation in this book will encourage you to run to Him and diligently pursue intimacy of relationship with the Father Who knows you perfectly and loves you anyway... and always.

He is a Good, Good Father. Jesus is the Way.

INTRODUCTION

Jesus said, *"I am the way and the truth and the life. No one comes to the Father except through me."*

If Jesus is "the way," there must be a destination! I used to think the destination was Heaven, but Jesus tells us the destination is the Father and He is the only way to get there.

The destination is not a place; it is a Person-God the Father. In Him is Life and Truth.

"Now this is eternal life: that they know you, the only true God, and Jesus Christ, whom you have sent." John 17:3

"... I have come that they may have life, and have it to the full." John 10:10b

"When the Advocate comes, whom I will send to you from the Father—the Spirit of truth who goes out from the Father—he will testify about me." John 15:26

It is not about religious rites, rules or rituals; rather, all truth and life is found in our intimacy of relationship with God the Father, because of the finished work of Jesus, through the Holy Spirit. Jesus Himself is the Way to the Father. Having a full life and living in the Truth begins when you are born again; and, it is experienced in an intimate personal relationship with the Father.

One of the primary purposes of Jesus coming to live among us was to show us the Father and provide a way for humanity to return to an intimate relationship with Him similar to what Adam and Eve had in the Garden before they sinned.

"Jesus makes God known to us as father. The Jews had known God as Yahweh for fourteen centuries, but the person who could introduce Him as Father was His Son." Derek Prince

"All this is from God [the Father], who reconciled us to himself through Christ and gave us the ministry of reconciliation: that God [the Father] was reconciling the world to himself in Christ, not counting people's sins against them. And he has committed to us the message of reconciliation." 2 Corinthians 5:18-19, bracketed comments mine

The word "father" is used about 350 times in the New Testament. Of these, I counted 265 times where the term "Father" is used in reference to God. About 70% of the time (192), it was Jesus speaking! Most of these 192 occurrences were the words of Jesus in Matthew (44) and in the Gospel of John (122). Jesus wanted His disciples to know the Father!

It is also very interesting that of the 122 times Jesus referred to the "Father" in the Gospel of John, 51 of those were the night before going to the Cross as recorded in John chapters 14-17. Jesus knew He was going to sacrifice His life the next day but the disciples still had not really put it all together.

A person who knows he will die the next day will very intentionally share the deepest matters of their heart with their loved ones.

They want their loved ones to remember the things that are most important, and they realize they will soon not have another opportunity to emphasize them. On this night, Jesus chose to tell His disciples primarily about the Father and the Holy Spirit. Whatever was important to Jesus should be important to us!

We are able by His Holy Spirit, through the finished work of Jesus at the Cross, to have an intimate personal relationship with God the Father! Isn't that amazing? As I consider it, I am so humbled and grateful that He loves us so much and simply desires us just to love Him in return. He longs for intimacy of relationship with us. This is almost unbelievable, but it is absolutely 100% true!

"In the Old Testament, the Israelites did not individually address God as Father. As far as we know Abraham, Joseph, Moses, David or Daniel never fell to their knees and dared to address God that way. Yet, in the New Testament, God is called Father over 260 times, and that is how we are instructed to speak to Him. All that a good father wants to be to his children, God will be to His children."
Haddon Robinson

As Christians, our goal and destination is relationship with God the Father; and we do not have to wait until we die. Truth and Life are available now. Jesus is the Way.

THE DESTINATION IS THE FATHER

J esus said, *"I am the way and the truth and the life. No one comes to the Father except through me."*

As earlier stated, if Jesus is "the way," there must be a destination! I used to think the destination was Heaven, but Jesus tells us the destination is the Father and He is the only way to get there.

It is not about religious rites, rules or rituals; rather, all truth and life is found in our intimacy of relationship with God the Father, because of the finished work of Jesus, through the Holy Spirit. Jesus Himself is the Way to the Father.

Why did Jesus need to show us the way? One of the primary reasons Jesus came was to restore a way back to relationship with God the Father similar to what Adam and Eve experienced in the Garden before they sinned. Theirs was a relationship of daily intimacy and communication with God. There was no barrier to experiencing each other and God one on one. They looked forward to walking and talking with God in the Garden of Eden in the cool of the day. It was only after their rebellion and sin that they hid themselves from God because of their newly found shame over their nakedness. See Genesis 3:8.

They believed the lie and suffered spiritual death. They no longer had access to the Tree of Life. Their way to relationship with the Father was lost. The Father sent Jesus so that we could have a way back to relationship with God the Father.

I find it really interesting that the disciples of Jesus were initially called followers of "The Way." Acts 9:2 tells us that Saul went to the Chief Priest *"and asked him for letters to the synagogues in Damascus, so that if he found any there who belonged to the Way, whether men or women, he might take them as prisoners to Jerusalem."* See also Acts 19:9; 19:23; 24:14 and 24:22.

Jesus is our best picture of the Father. Who better to show us the way? Jesus said, *"I and the Father are one"* (John 10:30). He also said, *"Anyone who has seen me has seen the Father"* (John 14:9). One of the primary reasons the Pharisees wanted to kill Him was that He made Himself equal to God. He could only tell the truth about His Father and they hated Him for it:

John 5:18-20 *"For this reason they tried all the more to kill him; not only was he breaking the Sabbath, but he was even calling God his own Father, making himself equal with God. Jesus gave them this answer: 'Very truly I tell you, the Son can do nothing by himself; he can do only what he sees his Father doing, because whatever the Father does the Son also does. For the Father loves the Son and shows him all he does. Yes, and he will show him even greater works than these, so that you will be amazed.'"*

Because of what Jesus did for us in His death, resurrection and ascension we can be born again into a new eternal family with God as our Father and pursue intimacy of relationship with Him. He loves us like He loved Adam and Eve, and like He loves Jesus!

In a devotional entitled "A Father's Love" Derek Prince wrote:

"God's family is the best family. Again, even if your own family did not care for you, bear in mind God wants you. You are accepted; you are highly favored; you are the object of His special care and affection. Everything He does revolves around you.

"Paul said to the Corinthians, who were not exactly top-notch Christians, *'All this is for your benefit'* (2 Corinthians 4:15 NIV). Everything God does, He does for us. You do not get conceited when you realize this fact. Instead, you become humble. There is no room left for arrogance when you see the grace of God. It is significant that, before His crucifixion, Jesus' last prayer with His disciples was for those who were His followers, as well as for those who would follow afterward. (See John 17:20). That prayer concerned our relationship with God as our Father, and it concluded, *'Righteous father, though the world does not know you, I know you, and they know that you have sent me. I have made you known to them.'* (John 17:25-26 NIV).

"Jesus makes God known to us as father. The Jews had known God as Yahweh for fourteen centuries, but the person who could introduce Him as Father was His Son. Six times in this prayer for His disciples, Jesus addressed God as Father (see verses 1, 5, 11, 21, 24, 25).

"When Jesus prayed, *'And [I] will continue to make you known'* (verse 26), He was saying that He would continue to reveal God as Father. Then, we come to the purpose of this revelation: *'In order that the love you have for me may be in them and that I myself may be in them.'* (John 17:26 NIV). God has exactly the same love for us as He has for Jesus. We are as dear to God as Jesus Himself is. However, there is another aspect to this. Because Jesus is in us, we can love God in the same way Jesus loves Him."

In a devotional at <u>www.first15.org</u> entitled "Seeing God as Father," Craig Denison concluded by writing:

"You are the child of a good, near and loving Father. Seeing God as your Father not only impacts your perception of Him but also of yourself. You are loved. You are liked. You are enjoyed. The God who only thinks, feels and says truth values relationship with you enough to send His only Son to die for you. Never let the world or the enemy shake the foundational love of your Heavenly Father. No failure, weakness or sin could ever change the fact that you are loved, accepted and valued. May you find peace today where there has only been loneliness, pressure and dissatisfaction."

Jesus is the way to the Father. Our designed destiny and destination is relationship with the Father.

Rev. J. Vernon McGee sums it up this way, "Jesus revealed and represented the Father before men. Now, He represents us before the Father. He took deity to this Earth and took mankind to Heaven."

Takeaway Highlight

Why did Jesus need to show us the way? One of the primary reasons Jesus came was to restore a way back to relationship with God the Father similar to what Adam and Eve experienced in the Garden before they sinned. Theirs was a relationship of daily intimacy and communication with God. There was no barrier to experiencing each other and God one on one. They looked forward to walking and talking with God in the Garden of Eden in the cool of the day. It was only after their rebellion and sin that they hid themselves from God because of their newly found shame over their nakedness. See Genesis 3:8.

They believed the lie and suffered spiritual death. They no longer had access to the Tree of Life. Their way to relationship with the Father was lost. The Father sent Jesus so that we could have a way back to relationship with God the Father.

Practical Application

Have you ever been traveling and thought you were lost? You might have needed help especially if it was before the days of GPS – Global Positioning System. You needed to find the right way and you realized you needed help. Think about other times in the past when you might have been wandering aimlessly through life unsure of your destination and how to get there. Maybe that describes you right now. Talk to God about Jesus being the way to the Father. Jesus is His GPS – God's Positioning System!

Jesus restored us to relationship through the Holy Spirit to the Father. How are the Father, Son, and Holy Spirit connected to One Another? Let's see...

THE CONCEPT
OF THE TRINITY
IN SCRIPTURE

Since this book examines the Scriptural references to the "Father," it seems important to consider the inter-relationships of the three Persons of the Godhead.

The word "Trinity" is not used in the Bible. The word is used to describe the Biblically disclosed truth that God is One in Three, and Three in One. The members of the Trinity – Father, Son and Holy Spirit – are co-existent, co-eternal, and co-equal. The Father is God, the Son is God, and the Holy Spirit is God, but they are distinct Persons from One another.

According to an article entitled "The Triune God" in the *David Jeremiah Study Bible*:

"One of the most important words in biblical theology was coined by the third-century Latin church father Tertullian: *trinitas*, or *Trinity* in English. The word *Trinity* does not occur in the Bible, but Tertullian used *trinitas* to communicate the relationship between Father, Son, and Spirit in Scripture.

"Perhaps the most helpful summary of the doctrine of the Trinity is this one by Princeton theologian B. B. Warfield: 'There is one only and true God, but in the unity of the Godhead there are three coeternal and coequal Persons, the same in substance but distinct in subsistence.'

"Ultimately, the doctrine of the Trinity depends on the fact that the Bible speaks of all three–Father, Son, and Spirit–as equally God and equal with each other. And although it remains a mystery beyond our human understanding, the truth of the Trinity is so clearly taught in Scripture that we can accept its implications on the basis of faith."

The Athanasian Creed, from the early Church fathers, put it this way: "We worship one God in Trinity...neither confusing the persons, nor dividing the substance...So the Father is God, the Son is God, and the Holy Spirit is God. And yet they are not three gods, but one God."

From an examination of the notes and articles in *The Life in the Spirit Study Bible*, the doctrine can be partially explained this way: "Each Person is uncreated, fully divine, equal with the other two, and eternal; yet they are not three Gods, but One."

A.W. Tozer, in his book, *Knowledge of the Holy*, has a chapter describing this truth as one attribute of God. This is my concise summary of the chapter on "The Holy Trinity":

The Bible reveals that there is one eternal God, with one essence, existing in three persons who are equal yet distinct: God the Father and God the Son and God the Holy Spirit. All three are together in unity, equal and co-eternal. They are both one and three. They have one will. They always work together, and not even the smallest thing is done by one without the instant agreement of the other two. Tozer said, *"The doctrine of the Trinity... is truth for the heart. The fact that it cannot be satisfactorily explained, instead of being against it, is in its favor. Such a truth had to be revealed; no one could have imagined it."*

From the RBC Ministries booklet *Do Christians Believe in 3 Gods?* there was posed this question: "Is it all right to address our prayers to Jesus or the Holy Spirit?"

Their answer: "We know that it is right and proper to pray to God the Father. Jesus told us to say, 'Our Father in heaven' (Matt. 6:9). We also know that we are to come to the Father in the name of Jesus, expecting Jesus to respond (Jn. 14:14). Stephen, at the moment of his death, addressed the Lord Jesus (Acts 7:59-60). We have no Bible passage that either directs us to pray to the Holy Spirit or gives us the example of doing so. However, we know that He is involved when we pray. Paul told us that the Spirit 'helps in our weakness' and 'makes intercession' when we do not know what to pray for (Rom. 8:26).

"It follows that we probably should address the Father when we pray. We should come in the name of Jesus. We should rely on the Holy Spirit to lead us in our praying. We should also depend on the Spirit to intercede for us when we don't know what to say.

We probably need not be unduly concerned about which Person we address. All three hear us when we pray. All are involved in the answers. Besides, no envy or jealousy exists within the Trinity."

The Holy Spirit is our friend, counselor, teacher and guide. In that capacity, although there is no exact scriptural illustration that we "pray" to the Holy Spirit, we are to experience His presence and have fellowship, commune, share and participate with Him as revealed in the Amplified Version of 2 Corinthians 13:14, *"The grace (favor and spiritual blessing) of the Lord Jesus Christ and the love of God and the presence and fellowship (the communion and sharing together, and participation) in the Holy Spirit be with you all. Amen (so be it)."*

Another question posed in the aforementioned RBC Ministries booklet was: "Can we use any illustrations to explain the doctrine of the Trinity?"

Their answer: "Probably not. I've seen people hold up an egg and say, 'The yolk, the white, and the shell make up the egg. This is three in one.' But the yolk is fat, the white is albumen, and the shell is calcium – no real unity. Some have said that water can exist as ice, liquid, and steam. But in any form, it is just water – not three in one. A minister thought he had a remarkable illustration when he said, 'I am a father to my family, a pastor to my church, and a citizen in my community – three in one.' But he was actually repeating the heresy that Father, Son, and Holy Spirit are three characteristics or modes or relations of the Godhead – three ways God works.

"The closest analogies probably can be found in these clusters of three: (1) in the universe – space, time and matter; (2) in matter – energy, motion, and phenomena; (3) in time – past, present, and future. But these analogies add little light to the subject of the Trinity. At best they may only *reflect* the three-in-oneness of the Creator."

RBC Ministries ended their booklet with this: "We must learn to live with a God we cannot fully comprehend. As C.S. Lewis has written: 'If Christianity was something we were making up, of course, we could make it easier. But it isn't. We can't compete, in simplicity, with people who are inventing religions. How could we? We're dealing with fact. Of course, anyone can be simple if he has no facts to bother about.'" (Quoted from *Beyond Personality: The Christian Idea of God*, by C.S. Lewis)

Perhaps the simplest explanation for the Trinity comes from Charles Colson, who described the Father, Son, and Holy Spirit as: "*God Above, God Beside, God Within.* We have a Father – God above us. We have a Savior – God beside us. We have a Spirit – God within us."

Additional Scriptural References

For a deeper dive into more specifics, here are some scriptures for further study summarized from the *Life in the Spirit Study Bible*:

1. Deuteronomy 6:4 declares that God is One, but it uses the plural form, Elohim. "Hear, O Israel: The Lord our God is one Lord..." (concerning God as One, see also Isaiah 45:21-22; 1 Corinthians 8:5-6; Ephesians 4:6; 1 Timothy 2:5).

2. The One essence we call "God" is manifested in three persons: Father, Son and Holy Spirit (Genesis 1:26; Matthew 28:19; 2 Corinthians 13:14; 1 Peter 1:2; Ephesians 4:6).

3. Some of the scriptures where each member of the Trinity is in evidence together: Matthew 28:19; Ephesians 2:18; 1 Peter 1:2; John 14:16; Romans 1:4; Acts 7:55; Hebrews 9:14; 1 John 5:7; John 15:6; Acts 10:38; Luke 1:35; Isaiah 61:1; 2 Corinthians 13:14; Matthew 3:16-17; Mark 1:9-11.

4. Jesus declares Himself equal with the Father (John 10:30). Thomas declared Jesus to be "Lord" (Greek = Kurios, meaning Supreme in authority) and "God" (Greek = Theos, meaning the Supreme deity) in John 20:28, and Jesus did not refute him, or correct him. In John 5:18-24, Jesus claims equality with God, and it is for this claim that the Pharisees declare Him blasphemous and want to kill Him. Other key scriptures where scripture declares Jesus as God, or speak of Him as having attributes only "God" can possess: John 1:1, 14; Colossians 2:9; Colossians 1:15-17; Hebrews 1:1-3, John 14:10-11; Isaiah 45:21-25.

5. The Holy Spirit is equated to God in Acts 5:3-4. In Matthew 10:20, Jesus refers to Him as the "Spirit of the Father." Paul refers to Him as the "Spirit of our God" in 1 Corinthians 6:11. The Holy Spirit is referred to as the "Spirit of God" in 1 Corinthians 2:11, Genesis 1:2 and Matthew 3:16.

Being Relational to God

The entire Bible is about "relationship," and Christianity has been defined as "not a religion, but a relationship." Being told that I need to have a relationship with God is intimidating and seems impossible. How can a material person have a relationship with an immaterial Spirit? Would it help me to understand and relate to what the Bible has revealed about the individual Persons of the One God?

I once asked the Holy Spirit to show me how I can be personally relational to God in each of His three persons. He showed me that, for me, I relate to God the Father in that I *trust* completely His sovereignty and almighty power to control all things. I relate to God the Son, Jesus, by the profound *love* I have for Him for all He did to reconcile me to God so that I have the opportunity to experience relationship with God, and receive the gift of eternal life. I relate to the Holy Spirit in the very humbling sense that I *need* Him in everything I do, every day.

I *trust* the Father; I *love* Jesus; and, I *need* the Holy Spirit. These are three ways I believe I can have a more intimate, personal relationship with God.

For more insight, see this book's chapter entitled "Relationship with Our Father."

I have previously shared what I am learning about having a relationship with Jesus in another book, *Knowing Jesus Intimately: A Relationship of Love-motivated, Spirit-empowered Obedience*. Additionally, since we all should want to be led by the Spirit daily instead of the flesh, I wrote *Knowing the One Who Leads You: 100 Days of Holy Spirit Fellowship*. You might want to later refer to these two titles for more about relationship with these persons of the Godhead.

Takeaway Highlight

The Bible reveals that there is one eternal God, with one essence, existing in three persons who are equal yet distinct: God the Father and God the Son and God the Holy Spirit. All three are together in unity, equal and co-eternal. They are both one and three. They have one will. They always work together, and not even the smallest thing is done by one without the instant agreement of the other two. A. W. Tozer said, "The doctrine of the Trinity... is truth for the heart. The fact that it cannot be satisfactorily explained, instead of being against it, is in its favor. Such a truth had to be revealed; no one could have imagined it."

Practical Application

Think about these two examples of the concept of three things in one. First, there is the Sun. It manifests as light, flame and heat all at once. Second, consider water. It can present itself as solid (ice), liquid, or gas (steam), albeit not all at the same time, but it is still water.

Let's begin to learn together what the Bible reveals about the Person of God the Father...

OLD TESTAMENT REFERENCES TO GOD AS "FATHER"

In the Old Testament, there are over 750 references to the word "father." In most cases it refers to genealogy. Interestingly, there are only seven instances I can find where the writer of scripture referred to God as "Father."

The Hebrews knew God as Provider, Protector, Healer, Shepherd and the like, but they did not really know God as "Father."

In the seven instances where Old Testament scripture refers to God as "Father," He is described as:

1. The Creator who made and formed us. (Deuteronomy 32:6)

2. The Potter who made us His handiwork. (Isaiah 64:8)

3. The Father and Creator of all. (Malachi 2:10)

4. A Judge to punish Israel for unfaithfulness and idolatry. (Jeremiah 3:4)

5. A shunned parent by his children. (Jeremiah 3:19)

6. The Everlasting Father. (Isaiah 9:6)

7. The Redeemer from of old. (Isaiah 63:16)

Since the Jewish family was such an important part of society, and fathers were so honored and respected, it surprised me to discover they did not seem to possess the revelation of, or emphasize their relationship to, God as "Father."

One of the main benefits for us as believers was that Jesus came to provide the opportunity for humanity to be restored to relationship with God the Father.

Takeaway Highlight

In the Old Testament, there are over 750 references to the word "father." In most cases it refers to genealogy. Interestingly, there are only seven instances I can find where the writer of scripture referred to God as "Father."

The Hebrews knew God as Provider, Protector, Healer, Shepherd and the like, but they did not really know God as "Father."

Practical Application

Look up each of the seven Scripture references above and consider what they are saying about God as Father.

As compared to the Old Testament, New Testament writers had a more complete revelation and understanding of God as Father...

NEW TESTAMENT REFERENCES TO GOD AS "FATHER"

J esus came to make it possible for humanity to again enjoy intimacy of relationship with God the Father similar to the closeness of relationship Adam and Eve experienced in the Garden before the Fall. As the Son, Jesus was perfectly positioned to reveal the Father. As stated in the previous chapter, knowing God as "Father" was not a concept generally understood or experienced at the time, yet it was something Jesus emphasized.

The word "father" is used about 350 times in the New Testament. Of these, I counted 265 times where the term "Father" is used in reference to God. About 70% of the time (192), it was Jesus speaking! Most of these 192 occurrences were the words of Jesus in Matthew (44) and in the Gospel of John (122). Jesus wanted His disciples to know the Father!

Paul definitely had the revelation of God as "Father" in that he used the term 41 times in his letters. The Apostle John used the term 22 times, primarily in his letter of 1 John. The other writers of the New Testament referred to God as "Father" 10 times.

It is also very interesting that of the 122 times Jesus referred to the "Father" in the Gospel of John, 51 of those were the night before going to the Cross as recorded in John chapters 14-17. Jesus knew He was going to sacrifice His life the next day but the disciples still had not really put it all together.

A person who knows he will die the next day will very intentionally share the deepest matters of their heart with their loved ones. They want their loved ones to remember the things that are most important, and they realize they will soon not have another opportunity to emphasize them. **On this night, Jesus chose to tell His disciples primarily about the Father and the Holy Spirit.** Whatever was important to Jesus should be important to us!

How was God the Father described by Jesus and the writers of the New Testament? I summarized them this way:

1. **We are His children and He loves us.**
   Matthew 5:45; 6:9; 23:9; Luke 11:2; John 14:20-21; 14:23-24; 16:25-28; 20:17; Romans 8:15; 2 Corinthians 6:18; Galatians 4:6; Ephesians 4:6; 1 Thessalonians 1:3; 3:11; 2 Thessalonians 2:16; 2 Peter 1:17; 1 John 2:14; 3:1; 5:1; Jude 1:1; Revelation 14:1.

2. **The Father desires a relationship with His children.**
   John 1:18; 10:15; 14:6; 16:3; Ephesians 2:18; 1 John 1:2-3; 2:15-16.

3. **It is possible for us to know Him.**
   Matthew 11:27; Luke 10:22.

4. **He is the source and sender of His Son, Jesus.**
   John 1:14; 5:36-37; 5:43; 6:57; 8:16; 8:41-42; 10:36-38; 12:26-28; 12:49-50; 13:3; 16:25-28; 20:21; 1 John 4:14.

5. **He is the Father of Jesus.**
   John 5:17-23; 8:18-19; 13:1; 2 Corinthians 11:31; Ephesians 1:2-3; Colossians 1:2-3; Hebrews 1:5; 5:5; 1 Peter 1:2-3; 2 John 1:3-4.

6. **He is equal to and one with Jesus.**
   John 5:17-23; 8:18-19; 10:29-30; 10:36-38; 14:6-13; 1 John 2:22-24; 5:1.

7. **The Father is to be glorified, praised and served.**
   Matthew 5:16; 16:27; Mark 8:38; Luke 9:26; John 12:26-28; 14:6-13; 15:8-10; 17:1; Romans 15:6; 2 Corinthians 1:2-3; Philippians 2:11; 4:20; James 3:9; Revelation 1:6.

8. **He is the ruler of and lives in the Kingdom of Heaven.**
   Matthew 26:29; Luke 12:32; 22:29; John 14:2; 14:6-13; 14:28; 16:10; 16:17; 16:25-28; 17:1; 20:17; 1 Corinthians 15:24; Revelation 3:21.

9. **He is worthy of worship, honor and thanksgiving.**
   Luke 2:49; John 4:21; 4:23; 5:17-23; 8:49; 14:28; 15:23-24; Ephesians 3:14; 5:20; Colossians 1:2-3; 1:12; 3:17.

10. **Our Father is worthy of and expects obedience.**
    Matthew 7:21; 12:50; John 12:26-28; 14:23-24; Hebrews 12:9; 1 John 1:9.

11. **He is holy and righteous in name and conduct.**
Matthew 6:9; Luke 11:2; John 17:11; 17:24-25; 1
Thessalonians 3:13.

12. **He is the example for, speaks to and teaches His Son.**
John 5:17-23; 8:27-28; 8:38; 12:49-50.

13. **The Father approves, glorifies and testifies of Jesus.**
John 5:36-37; 6:27; 8:18-19; 8:54; 17:1; 17:5; 2 Peter 1:17.

14. **He lives in and accompanies the Son.**
John 14:6-13; 14:20-21; 16:37; 17:21; 1 John 2:22-24.

15. **The Father assigns things to and for Jesus.**
Luke 10:21-22; 22:29; John 3:35; 5:17-23; 5:26; 5:36-37; 6:37.

16. **He commands or instructs the Son.**
John 10:17-18; 12:49-50; 14:23-24; 14:31; 15:8-10; 15:15-16;
18:11; Galatians 1:3-4.

17. **He gives us His Holy Spirit.**
Luke 11:13; 24:49; John 14:16; 14:26; 15:26; Acts 1:4; Acts
2:33; Ephesians 1:17.

18. **Our Father calls the lost to Jesus.**
John 6:37; 6:44; 6:65; 10:29-30; 17:24-25; Jude 1:1.

19. **He hears and answers our prayers.**
Matthew 18:19; 26:39; 26:42; Mark 14:36; Luke 22:42;
John 11:41; 14:16; 15:15-16; 16:23; 16:25-28.

20. **Our Father is the possessor and giver of life and eternal life.**
John 5:26; 6:40; 6:57; 17:3; 1 Peter 1:2-3; 1 John 1:2-3;
Revelation 3:5.

21. **He is the forgiver of sins.**
Matthew 6:14-15; Mark 11:25; Luke 23:34.

22. **The Father speaks, communicates and reveals.**
Matthew 10:20; 11:25-26; 16:17; Luke 10:21; John 6:44-46;
14:23-24; Ephesians 1:17.

23. **He is our provider and protector.**
Luke 12:30; John 6:32; 17:11; 1 Corinthians 8:6; James 1:27.

24. **He is the giver of gifts and fruit.**
Matthew 7:11; Luke 11:13; 12:32; John 15:15-16; 16:23;
1 Corinthians 8:6; James 1:17; 2 Thessalonians 2:16.

25. **He is the giver of love, grace and peace.**
Romans 1:7; 1 Corinthians 1:3; 2 Corinthians 1:2-3;
Galatians 1:3-4; Ephesians 1:2-3; 6:23; Philippians 1:2;
Colossians 1:2-3; 2 Thessalonians 1:1-2; 1 Timothy 1:2;
2 Timothy 1:2; Titus 1:4; 2 John 1:3-4.

26. **He is perfect.**
Matthew 5:48.

27. **Our Father sees everything.**
Matthew 6:4; 6:6; 6:18; 10:29.

28. **He knows everything.**
Matthew 6:8; 6:32; 24:36; Mark 13:32; Luke 12:30; John
10:15; 1 Peter 1:2-3.

29. **He possesses all power and never changes.**
Matthew 26:53; Acts 1:7; James 1:17.

30. **The Father is the giver of rewards.**
Matthew 6:1; 6:4; 6:6; 6:18; 20:23.

31. **He judges and holds people accountable.**
Matthew 10:32-33; Matthew 18:35; John 5:45; 1 Peter 1:17;
1 John 2:1.

32. **He blesses the righteous.**
Matthew 13:43; 25:34; Ephesians 1:2-3.

33. **He recognizes our efforts.**
Matthew 20:23; 25:34.

34. **Our Father is attended to, and surrounded by, Angels.**
Matthew 18:10; 26:53; Mark 8:38; Luke 9:26; Revelation
3:5.

35. **He loves children.**
Matthew 18:10; 18:14; Luke 2:49.

36. **He is active and working in the earth.**
John 5:17-23; 10:32; 10:36-38; 14:6-13.

37. **He loves the Son.**
John 3:35; 5:17-23; 15:8-10.

38. **Jesus sees the Father.**
John 6:44-46; 8:38.

39. **Jesus loves the Father.**
John 14:31.

40. **Our Father possesses His House, Temple and Church.**
Luke 2:49; John 2:16; 14:2; 1 Thessalonians 1:1;
2 Thessalonians 1:1-2.

41. **The Father shares all He has.**
John 16:15; Colossians 1:12.

42. **He gives authority.**
John 10:25; 13:3; 14:6-13; Revelation 2:27.

43. **He raises the dead.**
John 5:17-23; Romans 6:4; Galatians 1:1.

44. **He is a gardener.**
Matthew 15:13; John 15:1.

45. **He is a member of the Godhead trinity.**
Matthew 28:19.

46. **The Father comforts; and shows care, compassion and mercy.**
Matthew 10:29; Luke 6:36; 2 Corinthians 1:2-3.

47. **He receives us at death.**
Luke 23:46.

48. **Our Father provides power.**
Luke 24:49; John 17:11.

49. **Our Father instructs His children.**
2 John 1:3-4; 1:9

50. **He gives wisdom and revelation.**
Ephesians 1:17.

Take a few moments to review the list again. Meditate on their meaning and application as they apply to yourself and others. **Think about this... this is our Heavenly Father we are talking about as revealed through New Testament scriptural**

revelations! What an awesome God we serve. We are able by His Holy Spirit, through the finished work of Jesus at the Cross, to have an intimate personal relationship with Him! Isn't that amazing?

As I consider it, I am so humbled and grateful that He loves us so much and simply desires us just to love Him in return. He longs for intimacy of relationship with us. This is almost unbelievable, but it is absolutely 100% true! To Him be all praise, honor and glory!

Takeaway Highlight

Of the 122 times Jesus referred to the "Father" in the Gospel of John, 51 of those were the night before going to the Cross as recorded in John chapters 14-17. Jesus knew He was going to sacrifice His life the next day but the disciples still had not really put it all together.

A person who knows he will die the next day will very intentionally share the deepest matters of their heart with their loved ones. They want their loved ones to remember the things that are most important, and they realize they will soon not have another opportunity to emphasize them. On this night, Jesus chose to tell His disciples primarily about the Father and the Holy Spirit. Whatever was important to Jesus should be important to us!

Practical Application

Review all the Scriptures references above for the word "Father" in the order they appear in the New Testament by turning to page 117 where I have printed them out for you. Review them carefully. The Holy Spirit may show you some descriptions and attributes of the Father that I missed in the listing above!

Our Father has a very special place in His Heart for the outcasts, down trodden, rejected, abused, abandoned, lonely and forsaken. Whether a person is an "orphan" literally or figuratively, God is a Father to the fatherless. Read on...

A FATHER
TO THE
FATHERLESS

God's Word tells us that the fatherless and other neglected or abandoned children are very special to Him. God promises to give them His special favor, care, love and protection! Too many of us grow up without a father who is present, active and loving in our daily lives. Unfortunately, this happens because of divorce or death or because our father never married our mother.

Sometimes a father might be physically present at home, but emotionally and spiritually absent, because of work or misdirected worldly desires, addictions or other affections.

In some cases, we were raised by grandparents, foster parents, state institutions (or by "the streets" themselves) without the love, care or presence of *either* parent.

Regardless of the circumstances, this fact of life tragically affects too many. God does not cause these circumstances, but He is certainly aware of them and how they affect each of us.

His perfect will for us is to live *together* in a loving, Christian home as a whole family. When this is not possible, we are to call on God's promises. He will stand in for our earthly parents.

God wants us to come to Him for love, support and encouragement. He said, *"I will be a Father to you, and you will be my sons and daughters"* (2 Corinthians 6:18).

God knew each of us even before we were conceived by our parents. Our Heavenly Father has loved us even longer than our earthly parents. God said, *"Before I formed you in the womb I knew you, before you were born I set you apart..."* (Jeremiah 1:5a).

God has a special love and compassion for those who are neglected or abandoned or unloved. Psalm 27:10 says that God Himself will receive us when our mother or father forsake us. Also, Psalm 68:5 says that God will be *"a father to the fatherless."*

God's plans for us, and the number of our days on earth, are known by Him before we take our first breath. As our Heavenly Father, He thinks loving, kind and caring thoughts about us all the time; so many that they cannot even be counted! Psalm 139:13-18a expresses it this way:

"For you created my inmost being; you knit me together in my mother's womb. I praise You because I am fearfully and wonderfully made; Your works are wonderful, I know that full well. My frame was not hidden from You when I was made in the secret place. When I was woven together in the depths of the earth, Your eyes saw my unformed body. All the days ordained for me were written in Your book before one of them came to be. How precious to me

are Your thoughts, O God! How vast is the sum of them! Were I to count them, they would outnumber the grains of sand..."

Life without one or more of our earthly parents can be hard on us and is always unfortunate, whatever the reason. But, **take heart and be encouraged**, who better to "stand in" for your earthly parents than God, our Heavenly Father, the creator of the entire Universe!?! He wants to be your Father. Will you let Him?

Your Father knows you. He cares for you. He looks out for you. He loves you. You can depend on Him forever. *"He will never leave you or forsake you"* (Joshua 1:5). *"Cast all your cares on Him, for He cares for you."* (1 Peter 5:7).

Takeaway Highlight

God has a special love and compassion for those who are neglected or abandoned or unloved. Psalm 27:10 says that God Himself will receive us when our mother or father forsake us. Also, Psalm 68:5 says that God will be "a father to the fatherless."

God's plans for us, and the number of our days on earth, are known by Him before we take our first breath. As our Heavenly Father, He thinks loving, kind and caring thoughts about us all the time; so many that they cannot even be counted!

Practical Application

Have you ever felt unloved, rejected, ignored or abandoned? Study carefully Psalm 139 and think about how God our Father is able to fulfill us and meet our needs even when people do not. Choose to pursue Him. Accept Him as Father. Receive His Love.

Let me share with you a true example of the blessing of recognizing God as your Father...

A
FATHER'S
LOVE

As I was assembling material for this book I found an article I had saved from a number of years ago from a book someone shared with me, *God Allows U-Turns*, by Allison Gappa Bottke. It was reported to be a true story written by Michael T. Powers, Janesville, WS, entitled "A Father's Love." Grab a handkerchief; you may need it as you read:

"His name was Brian. He was a special education student at the small school I attended. He was constantly searching for love and attention. It usually came for the wrong reasons, from students who wanted to have some 'fun'. He was the joke of the school and was 'entertainment' for those who watched. Brian, who was looking for acceptance, didn't realize that they were laughing at him, not with him.

"One day, I couldn't take it anymore. I had enough of their game and told them to knock it off. 'Aw, come on, Mike! We are just having fun. Who do you think you are anyway!' The teasing didn't stop for long, but Brian latched onto me that day of my sophomore year. I had stuck up for him, and now he was my buddy. Thoughts of *What will people think of you if you are friends with Brian?* Swirled in my head, but I forced them away as I realized that God wanted me to treat this young man as I would want to be treated.

"Later that week, I invited him over to my house after school to play video games. We sat there playing Intellivision (this was the 80's) and drinking Tang. Pretty soon, he started asking me questions like, 'Hey, Mike, where do you go to church?' I would politely answer his questions, then turn my concentration back to the video games. He kept asking me questions about God and why I was different from some of the kids at school.

"Finally, my wonderfully perceptive girlfriend, Kristi, pulled me aside and said, 'Michael, he needs to talk. How about you go down to your room where you can talk privately?' She had picked up on the cues better than I had.

"As soon as we arrived in my room, Brian repeated, 'Hey, Mike, how come you're not like some of the other kids at school?' I knew I needed to share with him the difference that God had made in my life. I got out my Bible and shared John 3:16 and some verses in Romans with him. I explained to him that God loved him just the way he was and that he sent Jesus down to earth to die on a cross for him. All the while, I did not know if he was comprehending anything I was telling him. When we were done, I asked Brian if he wanted to pray with me. He said he would like that.

"We prayed together: 'God, I know I am a sinner, and that even if I were the only person on earth, You still would have sent Your Son down to die on a cross for me and take my place. I accept the gift of salvation that You offer, and I ask that You come into my heart and take control. Thank You, Lord. Amen.'

"I looked at him and said, 'Brian, if you meant those words you just prayed, where is Jesus right now?'

"He pointed to his heart and said, 'He is in here now.'

"Then he did something I will never forget, as long as I live. Brian hugged the Bible to his chest, lay down on the bed, and the tears flowed down his face. Brian was unearthly silent as the faucet behind his eyes let loose. Then he said to me, 'Mike, the love that God has for me must be like the love of a husband has for his wife.' I was floored.

"Here was someone who had trouble comprehending things in school, but who now understood one of eternity's great truths. I knew that he understood what I had shared with him.

"About a week later, everything came into perspective for me. It was then that Brian really opened up to me. He explained that his dad had left him and his mom when he was five years old. Brian was standing on the porch the day his dad told him he was leaving. He told Brian he couldn't deal with having a son like him anymore, then he walked out of Brian's life and was never seen again. Brian told me that he had been looking for his dad ever since.

"Now I knew why the tears kept flowing that day in my bedroom. His search was over. He found what he had been looking for since he was five years old. A Father's love.

"He would never again be alone."

Takeaway Highlight

"His name was Brian. He was a special education student at the small school I attended. He was constantly searching for love and attention. It usually came for the wrong reasons, from students who wanted to have some 'fun'. He was the joke of the school and was 'entertainment' for those who watched. Brian, who was looking for acceptance, didn't realize that they were laughing at him, not with him." Michael T. Powers

Practical Application

Have you ever known someone like Brian? Perhaps you even have been treated the way he was. Can you find yourself in this story? Have you surrendered to the Father's love? Stop. Think. Pray.

What if the Father wrote a letter to Brian? Or maybe one to you? How would you react to receiving a personal letter from God? Read on...

THE
FATHER'S
LOVE LETTER

The words you are about to read are true.

They will change your life if you let them.

For they come from the heart of God.

He loves you, and He is the Father

you have been looking for all your life ...

This is His love letter to you:

My Child,

You may not know me, but I know everything about you ~Psalm 139:1

I know when you sit down and when you rise up ~Psalm 139:2

I am familiar with all your ways ~Psalm 139:3

Even the hairs on your head are numbered ~Matthew 10:29-31

For you were made in my image ~Genesis 1:27

In me you live and move and have your being. ~Acts 17:28

For you are my offspring ~Acts 17:28

I knew you even before you were conceived ~Jeremiah 1:4-5

I chose you when I planned creation ~Ephesians 1:11-12

You were not a mistake, for all your days are written in my book ~Psalm 139:15-16

I determined the exact time of your birth and where you would live. ~Acts 17:26

You are fearfully and wonderfully made ~Psalm 139:14

I knit you together in your mother's womb ~Psalm 139:13

And brought you forth on the day you were born ~Psalm 71:6

I have been misrepresented by those who don't know me ~John 8:41-44

I am not distant and angry, but am the complete expression of love ~1 John 4:16

And it is my desire to lavish my love on you ~1 John 3:1

Simply because you are my child and I am your Father ~1 John 3:1

I offer you more than your earthly father ever could ~Matthew 7:11

For I am the perfect Father ~Matthew 5:48

Every good gift that you receive comes from my hand ~James 1:17

For I am your provider and I meet all your needs ~Matthew 6:31-33

My plan for your future has always been filled with hope ~Jeremiah 29:11

Because I love you with an everlasting love ~Jeremiah 31:3

My thoughts towards you are countless as the sand on the seashore ~Psalm 139:17-18

And I rejoice over you with singing ~Zephaniah 3:17

I will never stop doing good to you ~Jeremiah 32:40

For you are my treasured possession ~Exodus 19:5

I desire to establish you with all my heart and all my soul ~Jeremiah 32:41

And I want to show you great and marvelous things ~Jeremiah 33:3

If you seek me with all your heart, you will find me ~Deuteronomy 4:29

Delight in me and I will give you the desire of your heart ~Psalm 37:4

For it is I who gave you those desires ~Philippians 2:13

I am able to do more for you than you could possibly imagine ~Ephesians 3:20

For I am your greatest encourager ~2 Thessalonians 2:16-17

I am also the Father who comforts you in all your troubles ~2 Corinthians 1:3-4

When you are brokenhearted, I am close to you ~Psalm 34:18

As a shepherd carries a lamb, I have carried you close to my heart ~Isaiah 40:11

One day I will wipe every tear from your eyes ~Revelation 21:3-4

And I'll take away all the pain you have suffered on this earth ~Revelation 21:3-4

I am your Father, and I love you even as I love my Son, Jesus ~John 17:23

For in Jesus, my love for you is revealed ~John 17:26

He is the exact representation of my being ~Hebrews 1:3

He came to demonstrate that I am for you, not against you ~Romans 8:31

And to tell you that I am not counting your sins ~2 Corinthians 5:18-19

Jesus died so that you and I could be reconciled ~2 Corinthians 5:18-19

His death was the ultimate expression of my love for you ~1 John 4:10

I gave up everything I loved that I might gain your love
~Romans 8:31-32
If you receive the gift of my Son, Jesus, you receive me
~1 John 2:23
And nothing will ever separate my love from you
again ~Romans 8:38-39
Come home and I'll throw the biggest party that heaven
has ever seen ~Luke 15:7
I have always been Father and I will always be Father
~Ephesians 3:14-15
My question is...will you be my child? ~John 1:12-13
I am waiting for you ~Luke 15:11-32
Love, Your Dad, Almighty God

(Note: I do not know who first assembled all the above scriptures. If I could meet them I would surely thank them. My friend, Stephen Monk, found it in a trash can at the prison in Nashville where we were incarcerated together.)

Takeaway Highlight

This whole letter is the highlight! You might want to read it again.

Practical Application

Take some time to look up each of the Scriptures from which the phrases above were taken to understand the context surrounding the thought and it's complete wording. Share this letter with someone else who could use some love today.

The more we really begin to comprehend and receive the Father's love, we will want to pursue Him and seek Him with all of our heart. Primarily from scriptures in the Old Testament

we can learn the many ways the Jews knew and encountered God, and their Names for Him, even though they did not have the revelation of Him as the Father that Jesus revealed in the New Testament. Let's see what we can learn...

THE NAMES
OF GOD

Throughout the Bible, but primarily in the Old Testament, we learn of the different names the Jews used for God. By studying and learning their meanings we will continue to increase our understanding and appreciation of Father God.

The ministry of Dr. Adrian Rogers, Love Worth Finding, www. lwf.org, has continued to bless believers long after Dr. Rogers' graduation to Heaven in 2005. I found a great article he wrote on "The Names of God" that was very helpful to me. The information which follows comes from that article:

Abba ~ Father

"Have you ever thought about God as a daddy? Galatians 4:6 says, 'And because ye are sons, God hath sent forth the Spirit of his Son into your hearts, crying, Abba, Father.' Abba is the Aramaic word meaning Daddy, Father. It's a term of warm affection, intimacy, and respect for one's father. Now, to some that may sound like an irreverent way to address God, but Jesus called God, 'Our Father,' in Matthew 6:9 and He gave us that same right. In America, children call their fathers, Daddy. But in the Middle East, they say Abba. Jesus says that we can call the great God of the Universe, Abba Father. Daddy Father."

Related Scriptures–Mark 14:36; Romans 8:15; Galatians 4:6

Adonay ~ LORD, Master

"The gifted violinist Fritz Chrysler had a Stradivarius violin that at one time belonged to an old Englishman. Chrysler offered to buy it, but the old man told him that the violin was not for sale. One day he ventured to the old man's house and asked if he could touch it. The old man invited Chrysler in. He tucked it under his chin and began to draw the bow across the strings. Great tears began to well up in the old Englishman's eyes. Chrysler saw the man's face and said, 'I'm sorry, but I would so much like to buy this instrument.' The old Englishman said, 'It is not for sale, but it is yours. You are the master. You alone are worthy of it.' When we call God Adonay, we are saying that He is the Master. He alone is worthy, nothing and no one else. He is worth all that we have and all that we are."

Related Scriptures - Deuteronomy 10:17; Psalm 2:4, 8:1, 97:5, 136:3; Isaiah 1:24, 6:1; Romans 10:9

Alpha and Omega

"The noted historian, H. G. Wells, made a list of the ten greatest men of history and number one on that list was Jesus Christ. But, Jesus doesn't belong on that list. He doesn't belong on anybody's list. He is Jesus the First and the Last. Jesus said in Revelation, 'I am Alpha and Omega.' Alpha is the first letter of the Greek alphabet. Omega is the last. If Jesus was speaking to an English audience, He would say, 'I am A and Z.' Did you know that the Bible is made up of just twenty-six letters? What Jesus is saying about the written word is true about the living Word. John chapter one tells us that 'In the beginning was the Word... and the Word was made flesh, and dwelt among us.' Jesus was in the beginning as the Word of God. And He is God's final word for all eternity."

Related Scriptures – Revelation 1:8; 1:11; 21:6, 22:13

Attiyq Youm ~ The Ancient of Days

"What do you think about when you hear this name for God – 'Ancient of Days'? Isaiah 46:9-10 says, 'Remember the former things of old: for I am God, and there is none else; I am God, and there is none like Me, declaring the end from the beginning, and from ancient times the things that are not yet done, saying, My counsel shall stand, and I will do all My pleasure.' Only God can tell in ancient times the things that are not yet done. Thomas Watson, who was the chairman of IBM, said in 1943, that there's a world market for maybe five computers. In 1977 Ken Olsen, the founder of Digital Equipment, said, 'There's no reason anyone would want a computer in their home.' It's comments like these that help us see how foolish we are to think we can know the future. Only God is the Ancient of Days."

Related Scriptures - Daniel 7:9, 13, 14

Christos ~ The Anointed One

"First John 4:2 says, 'Hereby know ye the Spirit of God: Every spirit that confesseth that Jesus Christ is come in the flesh is of God.' John uses two names, Jesus, which refers to His human name, and Christ, which refers to His divine title. Jesus Christ is fully man and fully Messiah at the same time. Christ, which means Messiah, the Anointed One is His divine title. Jesus is God in human flesh. This is the fundamental doctrine of our faith - that God stepped out of heaven and took upon human flesh. We call that the incarnation. Carnis means flesh. When Jesus Christ took upon Himself humanity, He did not take it while He was here on earth and then laid it aside when He went back to heaven. He took His humanity back to heaven with Him. For all eternity Jesus Christ will be a man."

Related Scriptures - Matthew 1:16, 16:16-20; Mark 8:29; Luke 2:11, 9:20; John 1:41, 4:42, 6:69, 7:41-42, 11:27, 17:3, 20:31; Acts 2:36, 3:18, 5:42, 8:37, Romans 5:8, 5:15, 6:4, 6:23, 8:1, 8:39, 10:17; 1 Corinthians 1:30, 11:3, 12:12; 2 Corinthians 2:14-15, 5:17-20, 8:9, 12:9-10; Galatians 2:20-21, 6:14; Ephesians 1:5, 2:5-7, 4:15; Philippians 1:6, 1:21, 2:5-11, 3:7-9, 3:20, 4:19, Colossians 3:1-4; 1 Thessalonians 5:9; 1 Timothy 1:15-16, 2:5; Hebrews 3:6, 5:5, 9:14, 10:10, 13:8; 1 Peter 3:18; 1 John 5:6, 20; Revelation 11:15

El Chuwl ~ The God Who Gave You Birth

"Isaiah 43, 1-3b says, 'But now thus saith the LORD that created thee, O Jacob, and He that formed thee, O Israel, Fear not: for I have redeemed thee, I have called thee by thy name; thou art Mine. When thou passest through the waters, I will be with thee; and through the rivers, they shall not overflow thee: when thou walkest through the fire, thou shalt not be burned; neither shall the flame kindle upon thee. For I am the LORD thy God, the Holy One of Israel, thy Savior.' God is saying, 'I made you, I saved you, I'm going to take care of you.' God has made you for a purpose and He's going to take care of you. Even when sin marred God's original creation, God didn't say, 'I'm finished with it.' No. God made it and God stays with it. Isn't that a wonderful arrangement?"

Related Scriptures – Psalm 139:13-18

El Deah ~ God of Knowledge

"You think about His omniscience, He knows everything. God is the God of all knowledge. God inhabits eternity. God sees the beginning. God sees the middle. God sees the end. God sees it all at one time. God is all-knowing - He can't learn anything. God knows everything that's going to happen. Not a blade of grass moves but what He knows it. If you're saved, God knew that you would receive the Lord Jesus Christ. Nothing takes God by surprise. God never says, 'Ooops. I never thought of that.' God is omniscient. I don't understand how He swung the stars in the night sky. Or scooped the oceans and heaped up the mountains and runs this mighty universe. Romans 11:34 says, 'For who hath known the mind of the Lord? or who hath been His counsellor?' We don't have to know all that our Father does for Him to be our Father."

Related Scriptures - 1 Samuel 2:3; Romans 11:33-36; 1 Corinthians 1:18-31

El Elyon ~ The God Most High

"El Elyon speaks of the supremacy of God. He is above all. Now, what does El Elyon mean? The word means the strongest of the strong and the highest of the high. Hinduism and Pantheism speak of God as a part of the universe. But God is not a part of the universe. He is the transcendent God. He is above all. He is the Most High God. Jesus is our El Elyon. Colossians 1:16-17 says, 'For by Him were all things created, that are in heaven, and that are in earth, visible and invisible, whether they be thrones, or dominions, or principalities, or powers: all things were created by Him, and for Him: And He is before all things, and by Him all things consist.' God is above all things. Jesus is our El Elyon."

Related Scriptures - Genesis 14:18-20; Psalm 61:2; 92:1; Daniel 7:25

El Olam ~ The Everlasting God

"God never changes. Psalm 90:1-2 says, 'Lord, thou hast been our dwelling place in all generations. Before the mountains were brought forth, or ever thou hadst formed the earth and the world, even from everlasting to everlasting, thou art God.' What a wonderful thing to know that in a changing world God does not change! Time does not alter God. Psalm 90:4 says, 'For a thousand years in thy sight are but as yesterday when it is past, and as a watch in the night.' Well, what do all these verses mean? There are no surprises to God. As Corrie Ten Boom says, 'There's no panic in heaven.' God knows the past and the future at the same time. Jesus is our El Olam. He is the King of the Ages. Hebrews 1:8 says, 'But unto the Son He saith, Thy throne, O God, is for ever and ever: a sceptre of righteousness is the sceptre of thy kingdom.'"

Related Scriptures - Genesis 3:22; 21:33; Psalm 90:1-2; 93:2; Isaiah 9:6; 26:4; 40:28

El Roi ~ The God Who Sees

"El Roi was first revealed in the Bible by Hagar. She was Sarah's handmaiden, who became pregnant with Abraham's child so, in their minds, they could fulfill the promise of God. Soon after the child was conceived, things became very difficult between Sarah and her. So much so, that Hagar fled out into the wilderness. Friendless, homeless, pregnant, not knowing what would become of her, she laid down by a fountain in the wilderness. There, an angel appeared to her to give her comfort and to speak of God's grace and mercy. Genesis 16:13 says: 'And she called the name of the LORD that spake unto her, Thou God seest me: for she said, Have I also here looked after him that seeth me?' Did you know that God sees you right now? God knows your very thoughts. His eye is on the sparrow and I know He watches me."

Related Scriptures - Genesis 16:13; Genesis 16:1-16; Psalm 33:18-19

El Shaddai ~ God Almighty

"The name El Shaddai appears seven times in the Word of God. As I read the newspapers, I can go back to the Book of Genesis and see that immutable, unbreakable promise that God made to father Abraham. Genesis 17:1-2 says, 'And when Abram was ninety years old and nine, the LORD appeared to Abram, and said unto him, I am the Almighty God; walk before Me, and be thou perfect. And I will make My covenant between Me and thee, and will multiply thee exceedingly.' This promise has changed the world. Every Jew upon the face of the earth is a living testimony of the faithfulness of Almighty God. And this God who keeps His promise to Abraham is the same God that keeps His promises to you and I through Jesus Christ."

Related Scriptures - Genesis 17:1-19, 28:3; 35:11; 43:14; 48:3; Exodus 6:2-3; Ruth 1:20; Job 5:17; Ezekiel 10:5; Psalm 91:1

Elohim ~ The Creator

"Genesis 1:1 says, 'In the beginning God created the heaven and the earth.' It literally says, 'In the beginning Elohim, Elohim created the heaven and the earth.' That's the Hebrew word from two root words: El, which means strength and unlimited power. And the last part of is allah, which means to keep a promise. Elohim is also a plural noun. I believe that right here on the threshold of the Bible we see an indication of the nature of God, as shown in the Holy Trinity - God the Father, God the Son, and God the Holy Spirit. All three were present in creation (see John 1:3). Aren't you glad we find the Savior in chapter 1, verse 1? Aren't you glad we find the Holy Spirit in chapter 1, verse 1? Aren't you glad we find the Father in chapter 1, verse 1 of the Word of God?"

Related Scriptures - Genesis 1:1-3, 27-28; 3:3; Isaiah 40:28, 54:5; Psalm 19:1-6, 95:6; Nehemiah 9:17; Hebrews 1:8, 11:3

Yahweh ~ The Self-Existent One

"The name Jehovah is used some 6,800 times in the Bible. It is the personal covenant name of Israel's God. In the King James version of the Bible, it's translated Lord God. Not only does it speak of God's strength, but also it speaks of the sovereignty of God and the goodness of God. The root of this name means 'self-existing,' one who never came into being, and one who always will be. When Moses asked God, 'Who shall I tell Pharaoh has sent me?' God said, 'I AM THAT I AM.' Jehovah or Yahweh is the most intensely sacred name to Jewish scribes and many will not even pronounce the name. When possible, they use another name."

Related Scriptures - Isaiah 40:3; 10; 1 Samuel 1:20; Exodus 6:1-4; 3:1-22; John 6:35; 8:12; 10:7, 9, 11, 14; 11:25; 14:6; 15:1, 5

Yahweh-Bore ~ The LORD Creator

"Can you imagine what a modern writer would do if he tried to describe the creation of the heavens and the earth? Even if he believed in God, what an avalanche of adjectives he would pour out! What double-jointed and obtuse terms he would have to use to describe the creation of the earth! Aren't you glad that God said it, surely, sweetly, sublimely, and simply: 'In the beginning, God created the heavens and the earth.' How beautiful that is. It always tickles me when I read about how scientists are trying to discover the mystery of the creation of the universe. They just scratch their heads and say, 'We've got to go back to the laboratory now, a lot of things we thought we knew we didn't know.' God just spoke and it was so."

Related Scriptures - Genesis 1:1; Psalm 33:6; Isaiah 40:28-31; Job 38:1-41, 39:1-30, 40:1

Yahweh-Nissi ~ The LORD My Banner

"The Lord is a reigning banner over us all the time. The Hebrew for 'banner' comes from the root word 'to be high' or 'raised.' This was the name given to the altar that Moses erected to commemorate the defeat of the Amalekites at Rephidim (Exodus 17:8-15). He goes before us and behind us to give us the victory in all circumstances of life. Even in the midst of the battle, the banner of the Lord is raised over us. Psalm 23:5 says, 'Thou preparest a table before me in the presence of mine enemies: Thou anointest my head with oil; my cup runneth over.' Who is the God who prepares a table of celebration in the presence of the enemy? When the enemy shall come in like a flood, then shall the Lord hold up a banner before him. The victory in all of life is the Lord's."

Related Scriptures – Exodus 17:15

Yahweh-Raah ~ The LORD My Shepherd

"Psalm 23 and John 10 are the most beautiful descriptions of God as our Shepherd, Jehovah Rajah. When we say 'Lord,' we think of God's deity. When we say 'my Shepherd,' we think of God's humanity. God in human form - Jesus Christ - prophesized in the Old Testament and revealed in the New Testament. The Jehovah of the Old Testament is the Jesus of the New Testament. As the Good Shepherd, He dealt with the penalty of sin. As the Great Shepherd, He deals with the power of sin. As the Chief Shepherd, He's coming to take us from the very presence of sin."

Related Scriptures - Psalm 23; 80:1; 95:7; Isaiah 40:11; Jeremiah 31:10; Ezekiel 34:12; 23; Matthew 25:32; John 10:11-27; Hebrews 13:20-21; 1 Peter 2:25; 5:4

Yahweh-Rapha ~ The LORD That Healeth

"Does Jesus heal? Yes! He is the Almighty Lord, our healer. He can heal instantaneously by a miracle. He can heal over time through medicine. But let me add, that not every saint will be healed in this lifetime either by miracle or by medicine, nor instantaneously or in time. Right now, God is more interested in having you holy rather than healthy. Our bodies are not yet redeemed. The redemption of the body is going to come at the rapture of the church and the resurrection of the Christian dead. It is at that time that we will be made like unto Him. There is no sickness in the Lord's body and there will be no sickness in our resurrection body. If you are not healed in this life, child of God, you will be healed in eternity."

Related Scriptures - Exodus 15:26; 2 Chronicles 7:14; Psalm 6:2; 41:4; 103:3; 147:3; Isaiah 19:22; 30:36; 57:18-19; Jeremiah 3:22; 17:14; 30:17; Matthew 8:7; 10:1; Luke 4:18

Yahweh-Shalom ~ The LORD Is Peace

"The Lord greeted Gideon in peace, so he built an altar and named it 'The LORD is Peace' (see Judges 6:23-24). You have probably heard the blessing 'Shalom' from Jewish friends and acquaintances. It means peace. More importantly it means the Lord, our peace. Where does the Shepherd lead His sheep? Beside peaceful, still waters. 'He leads me beside the still waters;

He makes me lie down in green pastures' (Psalm 23:2). When your heart is content, you are at peace. And where does that contentment come from? The grace of God. There's no man more discontent than one who is not experiencing the amazing grace of God. Only in Jesus, will you find security, sufficiency, and serenity."

Related Scriptures - Genesis 49:10; Judges 6:23-24; Psalm 4:8; 29:11; Proverbs 16:7; Isaiah 26:3; 2 Thessalonians 3:16

Yahweh-Shammah ~ The LORD Is There

"Psalm 139:7 asks, 'Whither shall I go from Thy spirit? or whither shall I flee from Thy presence?' And what is the answer? God is omnipresent. He's everywhere. Somebody said that God is a circle whose center is everywhere and whose circumference is nowhere. There is not a murmur, but that He hears it. There's not a movement, but that He sees it. There's not a motive, but that He knows it. Neither Death, darkness, nor distance can hide us. When I am discouraged, His presence sees me through. When I am lonely, His presence cheers me up. When I am worried, His presence calms me down. When I am tempted, His presence helps me out."

Related Scriptures - Genesis 28:15; Ezekiel 48:35; Psalm 23:4; 46:1; 139:7-12; Jeremiah 23:23-24; Amos 5:14; Matthew 18:20; 28:20; John 14:16-17; Acts 7:48-49; 17:24-28

Yahweh-Tsabbaoth ~ The LORD Of Hosts

"Jehovah-sabaoth literally means the Lord Almighty. It speaks of the sovereignty of God over all the powers of the universe. The second stanza from Martin Luther's hymn 'A Mighty Fortress Is Our God' says, 'Did we in our own strength confide, Our striving would be losing, Were not the right man on our side, The man of God's own choosing. Dost ask who that may be? Christ Jesus, it is He, Lord Sabbaoth His name, From age to age the same, And He must win the battle.' David understood the greatness of God when he went against Goliath with five smooth stones and a sling. David said to Goliath, 'Thou comest to me with a sword, and with a spear, and with a shield: but I come to thee in the name of the LORD of hosts, the God of the armies of Israel, whom thou hast defied.' Oh, that each of us would have this same conception of God in our battles."

Related Scriptures - Isaiah 6:3; 1 Samuel 1:3, 17:45; 2 Samuel 6:2, 7:26-27; 1 Chronicles 11:9; Haggai 1:5; Romans 9:29; James 5:4; 2 Corinthians 6:18; Revelation 1:8; 4:8

Yahweh-Tsidkenu ~ The LORD Our Righteousness

"We are not righteousness in and of ourselves. Our righteousness comes from God and God alone. Jesus imputes His righteousness into us so that we can see God. For you see, Hebrews 12:14 says that without holiness, no man will see God. Second Corinthians 5:21 says, 'For he hath made him to be sin for us, who knew no sin; that we might be made the righteousness of God in him.' Isn't that terrific? You see, if you are a child of God, you are holy. Are you feeling that you can't live the Christian life? That's right where you need to be. You see, God never asked you to live the Christian life apart from Him. He wants to be your strength, He wants to live the Christian life through you and do for you what you could never do for yourself."

Related Scriptures - Genesis 15:6; Jeremiah 23:6; Psalm 4:1; 5:8; 24:5; 31:1; 36:10; 71:15; 89:16; Matthew 6:33; Romans 4:22; 5:18; 8:10; 10:4; 1 Corinthians 1:30; 2 Corinthians 5:21; Philippians 3:9

Yahweh-Yireh ~ The Lord Will Provide

"Yireh is from the same Hebrew word as Moriah, which is the name of the region where God sent Abraham to sacrifice Isaac (Genesis 22). In Genesis 22:11-13 we read, 'And the angel of the LORD called unto him out of heaven, and said, Abraham, Abraham: and he said, Here am I. And he said, Lay not thine hand upon the lad, neither do thou any thing unto him: for now I know that thou fearest God, seeing thou hast not withheld thy son, thine only son from me. And Abraham lifted up his eyes, and looked, and behold behind him a ram caught in a thicket by his horns: and Abraham went and took the ram, and offered him up for a burnt offering in the stead of his son.' God provided the lamb. And Abraham called the place Yahweh-Yireh - God is our substitutionary sacrifice."

Related Scriptures - Genesis 22:14, 22:1-18

Takeaway Highlight

"Have you ever thought about God as a daddy? Galatians 4:6 says, 'And because ye are sons, God hath sent forth the Spirit of his Son into your hearts, crying, Abba, Father.' Abba is the Aramaic word meaning Daddy, Father. It's a term of warm affection, intimacy, and respect for one's father. Now, to some that may sound like an

irreverent way to address God, but Jesus called God, 'Our Father,' in Matthew 6:9 and He gave us that same right. In America, children call their fathers, Daddy. But in the Middle East, they say Abba. Jesus says that we can call the great God of the Universe, Abba Father. Daddy Father." Dr. Adrian Rogers

Practical Application

Choose one or two of God's Names as summarized above to meditate upon each day. Include it as a matter of prayer and worship in your quiet time with God. Be intentional about getting to know Him better.

In addition to what we are learning about the Names of God and the ways He has manifested Himself, there are other attributes of God that have been also derived from Scripture that will enable us to worship Him in spirit and in truth. Read on...

KNOWLEDGE
OF THE
HOLY ONE

We are drawn ever closer to God the Father in relationship as we get to know Him better. He is Holy.

"The fear of the LORD is the beginning of wisdom, and knowledge of the Holy One is understanding." Proverbs 9:10

As we gain more wisdom, knowledge and understanding of the Father our true worship of Him increases.

"Yet a time is coming and has now come when the true worshipers will worship the Father in the Spirit and in truth, for they are the kind of worshipers the Father seeks. God is spirit, and his worshipers must worship in the Spirit and in truth." John 4:23-24

To worship Him in spirit and in truth, we must come to the Father in complete sincerity. Our own spirit must be directed by the Holy Spirit within us. Worship must take place according to the truth that is revealed in the Son and received through the Holy Spirit.

To truly worship Him in spirit and truth we must gain knowledge and understanding of Him. God has revealed certain truths about Himself to us which we can begin to understand by reading His Word. In addition, we know Jesus is the Living Word, and we see His example for us. We also learn about God through His Holy Spirit who resides in us teaching us about His qualities and attributes.

"We can understand the attributes of God in other ways, but we can only understand the Father's heart in the Cross of Christ"
Oswald Chambers

God knows we cannot truly understand the Infinite with our comparatively feeble, finite brains. We can only begin to fathom some of His qualities and attributes through Spirit-inspired Word into our hearts. In this body on earth, we will never know or fully understand everything about Him. But as we seek Him diligently daily, He gradually reveals Himself to us. It is out of a deep knowing in our hearts, not the thoughts of our mind, that we are able to begin to truly worship Him in spirit and in truth.

As you begin to better appreciate the awesomeness, vastness and holiness of God, you will develop a different perspective of yourself and the challenges or problems you face daily. London Pastor F.B. Meyer once wrote, "The best answer to self-consciousness is God-consciousness. When I concern myself, not with the perceived inequities and injustices I face but rather with ministering the things that matter to God, I find myself feeling abundantly privileged and blessed. What changed? It was my vision. The surest way to lift a person's spirit is to lift his focus."

Pastor Meyer continues, "When I look, not only to the things of God, but to God Himself, I find that I have more reasons to rejoice than I have to mourn. I possess more than I've lost. I have more in my hand than has slipped through my fingers. I have more to thank God for than to petition Him for."

I summarized the following information about some of God's attributes from A. W. Tozer's book entitled *The Knowledge of the Holy*. As you prayerfully review these attributes, be careful to meditate on their meaning. Stop to appreciate their truth. Ask His Spirit to increase your knowledge and understanding of Him. When you pray during your daily quiet times, be sure to acknowledge and praise Him in light of His revelation to you of these truths describing His Holy nature and character. Your increased knowledge of the Holy One will enable you to worship and adore Him more fully.

A.W. Tozer, in his book, *The Knowledge of The Holy*, wrote,

"What comes into our minds when we think about God is the most important thing about us... The most important fact about any man is not what he at a given time may say or do, but what he in his deep heart conceives God to be like...Without doubt, the mightiest thought the mind can entertain is the thought of God...We can never know who or what we are till we know at least something of what God is...For while the name of God is secret and His essential nature incomprehensible, He in condescending love has by revelation declared certain things to be true of Himself. These we call His attributes."

Some Attributes of God (summarized from *The Knowledge of The Holy*, by A. W. Tozer):

The Holy Trinity - The Bible reveals that *there is one eternal God, with one essence, existing in three persons who are equal yet distinct: God the Father and God the Son and God the Holy Spirit.* All three are together in unity, equal and co-eternal. They are both one and three. They have one will. They always work together, and not even the smallest thing is done by one without the instant agreement of the other two. Tozer said, "The doctrine of the Trinity... is truth for the heart. The fact that it cannot be satisfactorily explained, instead of being against it, is in its favor. Such a truth had to be revealed; no one could have imagined it."

The Self-existence of God – *God has no origin.* Origin is a word that can apply only to things created. God was not created. He is self-existent. Aside from God, nothing is self-caused. Tozer writes, "Everything was made by Someone who was made of none...Man is a created being...who of himself possesses nothing but is dependent each moment for his existence upon the One who created him after His own likeness."

The Self-sufficiency of God – *God requires no helpers and has no needs.* God is what He is in Himself. All life is in and from God. Nothing is above Him. Nothing is beyond Him. Man is not necessary to God. He is not greater because we exist and He would not be less if we did not exist. God does not need our help. He does not need us to defend Him or His truths. His truth would still exist without us. God exists for Himself and man exists for His glory.

The Eternity of God – *He is endless and everlasting.* Time marks the beginning of created existence, and because God was not created and never began to exist, time has no application to Him. He exists above and outside of time. Because God lives in an everlasting now, He has no past or future. When time-words occur in Scripture they refer to our time, not to His. God dwells in eternity, but time dwells in God. Time began in God and it will end in Him.

God's Infinitude – *God has no limits in any thing or in any way.* Infinitude means limitless. Unfortunately, it is impossible for a limited mind to understand the unlimited. God is greater than mind itself. His greatness cannot be conceived. He knows no bounds. He is without limit. He cannot be measured. He is above, outside and beyond measurement. Because God's nature is infinite, everything that flows out of it is infinite also – for example, His love, grace, mercy and justice. Those who are in Christ share with Him all the riches of limitless time and endless years. God never hurries.

The Immutability of God – *God does not change.* God never differs from Himself. He cannot change for the better. For example, since He is perfectly holy, he has never been less holy than He is now and can never be holier than He is and has always been. Similarly, neither can God change for the worse. Any deterioration within the holy nature of God is impossible. Nothing that God has ever said about Himself will ever be modified or rescinded. In all our efforts to find God, commune with Him and to please Him, we must remember that we must be the ones who change. God won't.

The Divine Omniscience – *God knows all things perfectly and equally well.* God possesses perfect knowledge and therefore has no need to learn. In fact, God has never learned and cannot learn. Since God is the source of all things, He knows all that can be known, instantly and effortlessly. He knows all things equally well. He never discovers any other thing. He is never surprised, never amazed and never wonders. God knows us completely. He knew us before we knew Him and He called us to Himself in the full knowledge of everything that was against us. No weakness in our character can ever come to light to turn God away from us. Whatever happens to us, God knows and cares as no one else can.

The Wisdom of God – *His wisdom is perfect and infinitely pure, loving and good.* His understanding is infinite. The idea of God as infinitely wise is at the root of all truth. Wisdom sees everything clearly, in proper relation to everything else. All God's acts are done in perfect wisdom, first for his own glory, and then for the highest good of the greatest number of people for the longest time. No matter how things may look, all God's acts are done in His perfect wisdom. We can count on God to know and do what's best.

The Omnipotence of God – *God has all power – limitless and absolute.* Omnipotent means having all power. The Bible often uses the more familiar word Almighty, but it is used only of God. He alone is almighty. God is infinite, without limit. Therefore God has limitless power. Nothing is too hard or difficult for God because He possesses absolute power, having command of all power in the universe.

The Divine Transcendence – *His Being is exalted infinitely above all other being*. This means that God is exalted far above the created universe, so far above that human thought cannot imagine it. "Far above" does not refer to physical distance but to quality of being. God is Spirit, and to Him magnitude and distance have no meaning. Forever God stands apart. It is God Himself who puts it into our hearts to seek Him and makes it possible in some measure to know Him, and He is pleased with even our feeblest efforts to make Him known to others.

God's Omnipresence – *God is everywhere here, close to everything, next to everyone*. In His presence is fullness of joy! God pervades His creation. There is no place in heaven or earth where men may hide from His presence. The Scriptures teach that God is at the same time far off and near, and that in Him men move and live and have their very being. Since He is infinite, there is no limit to His presence; He is omnipresent. God surrounds His finite creation and contains it. There is no place beyond Him for anything to be. God is near us, next to us, and He sees us through and through. Through Jesus Christ He is immediately accessible at all times to every loving and believing heart. The knowledge that we are never alone calms the troubled sea of our lives and speaks peace to our souls.

The Faithfulness of God – *God is true to His Word. His promises are always honored*. All of God's acts are always consistent with every one of His attributes. No attribute contradicts any other, but all harmonize and blend with each other. All that God does agrees with all that God is, He cannot act out of character with Himself. He is at once faithful and immutable, so all His words and acts must be and must remain faithful. There is no conflict among the divine attributes. God's being is unitary. He cannot divide Himself and act at any given time from one of His attributes while the rest remain inactive. All that God is must be in accord with all that God does. Justice must be present in mercy, and love in judgment. This is true with all His attributes. Because He is faithful, we are able to live in peace and look forward with assurance to all He has promised us here on earth, and later in eternity with Him.

The Goodness of God – *He is infinitely kind and eternally blessing without partiality.* The goodness of God is what disposes Him to be kind, cordial, benevolent and full of good will toward men. He is tenderhearted and quick in sympathy. He is always open, frank and friendly. By His very nature He is inclined to bestow blessings and He takes pleasure in the happiness of His people. God created us because He felt good in His heart and He redeemed us through Jesus for the same reason. The unmerited, spontaneous goodness of God is behind His every act of grace. His Divine goodness is self-caused, infinite, perfect, and eternal. Since God is immutable He has never been kinder than He is now, nor will He ever be less kind.

The Justice of God – *God's judgment is His application of equity to moral situations, and may be favorable or unfavorable.* The words for justice and righteousness as applied to God are used interchangeably in Scripture. They are forever intertwined. Justice embodies the idea of moral equity (or "rightness"), and iniquity is exactly the opposite; it is in-equity, the absence of equality from human thoughts and acts. Justice, when used of

God, is a name we give to the way God is, nothing more; and when God acts justly He is simply acting like Himself in a given situation. Everything in the universe is good to the degree it conforms to the nature of God, and evil as it fails to do so. God is able to supply us mercy and compassion as sinners only because His justice was fully and forever satisfied when Jesus took all our sins away on the cross. In God's eyes, Jesus took our sins and gave us His righteousness. This is known as "the great exchange." However, God's justice stands forever against the unrepentant sinner. It can never be any other way.

The Mercy of God – *This is God's pity and compassion for human suffering and guilt.* We really have no right to ever enter Heaven. Yet, it is by God's mercy that we who have earned banishment shall instead enjoy communion with God in His presence; we who deserve the pains of hell shall know the bliss of Heaven. His mercy is His infinite and inexhaustible energy within His divine nature that causes Him to be actively compassionate. But we must realize He is just (full of justice) as well as merciful. He has always dealt in mercy with mankind, and will always deal in justice when His mercy is rejected and despised.

The Grace of God – *Grace is His infinite goodness and unmerited favor directed towards human debt and demerit, given to us along with the power to do His will.* It is the good pleasure of God to bestow benefits on the undeserving. It comes from the very heart of God, but the channel through which it flows out to us is Jesus Christ, crucified and risen! We who feel ourselves alienated from the fellowship of God can now raise our discouraged heads and look up. Through Christ's atoning death the cause of our banishment has forever been removed.

The Love of God – *God's love is His eternal uncaused and undeserved good will to all.* The words the Apostle John wrote, "God is love," mean that love is an essential attribute of God. Love is something true of God but it is not God. It expresses the way God is in His unitary being, as do the words holiness, justice, faithfulness and truth, but it is not all He is. His love always operates in harmony with all of His other attributes. He does not suspend one to exercise another. We may never know entirely what love is, but we can know it in the way it manifests itself. God shows us His love in His good will. Love wills the good of all and never wills harm or evil to any. Because of His holiness and righteousness, God hates sin and can never look with pleasure on iniquity, but where men in Christ seek to do God's will He responds in genuine affection.

The Holiness of God – *His holiness is His infinite purity, moral excellence and absolute righteousness.* No human can ever be qualified to fully appreciate or understand the holiness of God. We know nothing like it and have nothing to acceptably compare it with. It stands apart, unique, unapproachable, incomprehensible and unattainable. We may fear His power and admire His wisdom, but His holiness we cannot even imagine. Only His Spirit can impart to us the knowledge of the holy. Holy is the way God is. To be holy He does not conform to an objective standard. He is that standard. He is absolutely holy with an infinite, incomprehensible fullness of purity that is incapable of being other than it is. We must hide our un-holiness in the wounds of Christ. We must take refuge from God in God. We must believe that God sees us perfect in His Son and thereby allows us to be partakers of His holiness.

The Sovereignty of God – *Sovereignty refers to God's absolute authority everywhere, forever.* God's sovereignty is the attribute by which He rules His entire creation, and to be sovereign God must be all-knowing, all-powerful, and absolutely free. No one and no thing can hinder Him or compel Him or stop Him. He is able to do as He pleases always. In the moral conflict that rages constantly around us, whoever is on God's side is on the winning side and cannot lose; whoever is on the other side is on the losing side and cannot win. There is freedom to choose which side we shall be on but no freedom to negotiate the results of the choice once it is made. By the mercy of God we can repent a wrong choice and alter the consequences by making a new and right choice. We must all choose whether we will obey the gospel or turn away in unbelief and reject its authority. Our choice is our own, but the consequences of the choice have already been determined by the sovereign will of God, and from that there is no appeal.

The Knowledge of the Holy

The best counsel one can receive and implement is to "acquaint thyself with God." Our prayer life and relationship with God will be enriched as we meditate on His attributes. As we more fully understand His true nature and greatness we will naturally and enthusiastically worship, praise and adore Him in our daily quiet times with Him. Our faith will grow. Our witness will be more effective. We will remain humbly grateful.

As the knowledge of God becomes more real and wonderful to us we will feel a need for greater service to our fellow man. This blessed knowledge comes through the Holy Spirit pouring truth into our hearts, and such knowledge is not given to be enjoyed selfishly. The God who gave all *to* us will continue to give all *through* us as we come to know Him better. We must seek purposefully to share our increasing light with the fellow members of the household of God, and live in such a way that others may be brought out of darkness.

Remember: Stand in awe of God. Meditate on His beauty, wisdom, and love. Then praise Him!

Join me in praying: *Oh Lord, I choose to trust in who You are rather than who I am. In Jesus' Name. Amen.*

Related Scriptures – Proverbs 9:10-11; John 4:23-24; 1 Corinthians 13:11-13; Psalm 93:1-2; 1 Chronicles 16:27; 1 Chronicles 29:11

Takeaway Highlight

To truly worship Him in spirit and truth we must gain knowledge and understanding of Him. God has revealed certain truths about Himself to us which we can begin to understand by reading His Word. In addition, we know Jesus is the Living Word, and we see His example for us. We also learn about God through His Holy Spirit who resides in us teaching us about His qualities and attributes.

God knows we cannot truly understand the Infinite with our comparatively feeble, finite brains. We can only begin to fathom some of His qualities and attributes through Spirit-inspired Word into our hearts. In this body on earth, we will never know or fully understand everything about Him. But as we seek Him diligently daily, He gradually reveals Himself to us. It is out of a deep knowing in our hearts, not the thoughts of our mind, that we are able to begin to truly worship Him in spirit and in truth.

Practical Application

Choose one or two of God's attributes as summarized above to meditate upon each day. Include them as a matter of prayer and worship in your quiet time with God. Be intentional about getting to know Him better.

When one considers the above attributes of God, and the majesty of His Names in the last chapter, we are better prepared and motivated to praise Him; and, to foster a respectful, holy and reverent fear of the Lord. Let's learn more...

THE FEAR
OF THE LORD

The biggest problem in our country is not inflation, illegal immigration, drugs, sexual immorality and the like; it is that there is very little of a proper fear of God. The majority of people seem to have lost their awe, reverence and respect for God Almighty; but the fear of the Lord is crucial for a personally intimate relationship with our Father.

What is the fear of the Lord?

Fear of the Lord is having a deep awe, reverence, and respect for Him; and a healthy fear of doing anything that would displease Him. It is honoring God as God because of His great glory, holiness, majesty and power. It is the result of a deep appreciation of our own nothingness and of the infinite greatness and majesty of God. It stands opposed to pride and self-confidence.

For believers, it is not a fear that God will ever judge them for their sin (John 5:24; Romans 8:1). However, all God's children should possess a holy fear that trembles at the Word of God and causes them to turn away from evil.

"The person who fears God need not fear anything else; but the person who does not fear God is vulnerable to fearing everything else." Donald C. Stamps

In *Our Daily Bread*, they wrote, "To 'fear' the Lord God is to give Him the highest respect. For the believer, it is not a matter of feeling intimidated by Him or His character. But out of respect for His Person and authority, we walk in all His ways and keep His commandments. Out of 'love', we serve Him with all our heart and with all our soul – rather than merely out of duty. Love flows out of our deep gratitude for His love for us, rather than our likes and dislikes. 'We love Him because He first loved us' (1 John 4:19)."

Along with awe, reverence and respect for Him, we will have a humble, submissive attitude as an expression of having the fear of the Lord in our lives. When we are arrogant, conceited, self-sufficient and self-proclaiming there is no evidence of the true fear of the Lord in us.

"I believe that the reverential fear of God mixed with love and fascination and astonishment and admiration and devotion is the most enjoyable state and the most purifying emotion the human soul can know." A. W. Tozer

What Does it Mean to Fear God?

R. C. Sproul, answered this question in an article with the same title dated January 12, 2018:

"We need to make some important distinctions about the biblical meaning of 'fearing' God. These distinctions can be helpful, but they can also be a little dangerous. When Luther struggled with that, he made this distinction, which has become somewhat famous: he distinguished between what he called a servile fear and a filial fear.

"The servile fear is a kind of fear that a prisoner in a torture chamber has for his tormentor, the jailer, or the executioner. It's that kind of dreadful anxiety in which someone is frightened by the clear and present danger that is represented by another person. Or it's the kind of fear that a slave would have at the hands of a malicious master who would come with the whip and torment the slave. Servile fear refers to a posture of servitude toward a malevolent owner.

"Luther distinguished between that and what he called filial fear, drawing from the Latin concept from which we get the idea of family. It refers to the fear that a child has for his father. In this regard, Luther is thinking of a child who has tremendous respect and love for his father or mother and who dearly wants to please them. He has a fear or anxiety of offending the one he loves, not because he's afraid of torture or even of punishment, but rather because he's afraid of displeasing the one who is, in that child's world, the source of security and love.

"I think this distinction is helpful because the basic meaning of fearing the Lord that we read about in Deuteronomy is also in the Wisdom Literature, where we're told that the 'fear of the Lord is the beginning of wisdom'. The focus here is on a sense of awe and respect for the majesty of God. That's often lacking in contemporary evangelical Christianity. We get very flippant and cavalier with God, as if we had a casual relationship with the Father. We are invited to call Him Abba, Father, and to have the personal intimacy promised to us, but still we're not to be flippant with God. We're always to maintain a healthy respect and adoration for Him.

"One last point: If we really have a healthy adoration for God, we still should have an element of knowledge that God can be frightening. 'It is a frightening thing to fall into the hands of the living God' (Hebrews 10:31). As a sinful people, we have every reason to fear God's judgment; it is part of our motivation to be reconciled with God."

"The fear of God is a choice in that it involves the decision of our will to respond to the gracious invitation of God's Word and Spirit. Only as we truly fear the Lord will we be delivered from slavery to all abnormal and demonic fear." From *Life in the Spirit Study Bible* article, "The Fear of the Lord"

David Jeremiah, in a devotional entitled "Why Fear God?" wrote:

"Christians don't fear God because He knows we've sinned. Instead, we fear Him (adore Him, worship Him) because He forgave our sins.

"If you haven't accepted God's gift of forgiveness through faith in Christ, you have reason to fear His judgment. Accept His gift and stand in awe of Him instead."

Descriptions of the Fear of the Lord in Our Lives

Derek Prince wrote, "One of the best words to describe the fear of the Lord is reverence. Reverence is a response to a revelation of God. When God reveals Himself, I believe the only appropriate response is reverence. And with it goes submissiveness. A submissive attitude towards God is an expression of the fear of the Lord in our lives."

When we have this kind of daily attitude and respect for the Lord we are in a position to receive everything God has for us. In fact, our Father wants to share His treasure with us! *"He will be the sure foundation for your times, a rich store of salvation and wisdom and knowledge;* **the fear of the LORD is the key to this treasure."** (Isaiah 33:6, emphasis mine)

Derek Prince stated, "The fear of the Lord is often referenced in the Bible, but little understood by man – especially believers. Yet, we are told in the scripture above that it is the key to the treasure of God - His salvation, wisdom and knowledge!"

Andrew Wommack, in an article entitled "The Fear of the Lord," wrote this:

"If I was to quote the part of 1 John 4:18 that says perfect love casts out fear, I imagine I would get a hearty 'Amen!' from nearly all of you. **But if fear is a bad thing, then what do you do with the 300-plus scriptures that speak of fearing the Lord in a positive way?**

"For instance, Isaiah 11:1-2 says,

"And there shall come forth a rod out of the stem of Jesse, and a Branch shall grow out of his roots: And the spirit of the Lord shall rest upon him, the spirit of wisdom and understanding, the spirit of counsel and might, the spirit of knowledge and of <u>the fear of the Lord</u>. (underline mine).

"This is speaking of Jesus fearing His Father. He certainly didn't dread His Father, nor was He terrified of His judgment. But He honored, revered, trusted, loved, and submitted to His Father. The early New Testament church walked in the fear of the Lord (Acts 9:31). That is the positive fear of the Lord that I want to talk to you about.

"If it was important for Jesus and the early believers to fear God, then it would be a good idea for us to learn what the fear of the Lord really is."

The fear of the Lord is not what our natural man feels in the daily pressures and circumstances of life. As we survey the current state of our world today, it seems God's last days' judgment has begun and people are fearful of all kinds of things. This kind of fear is negative and destructive.

Proverbs 14:26 says, "In the fear of the Lord there is strong confidence." About this verse, Derek Prince wrote, "The fear of the Lord doesn't make you timid. It doesn't make you weak. The fear of the Lord gives you strength. When you fear the Lord you don't have to fear anything else. It's the remedy for all other ungodly forms of fear."

David Wilkerson, in his devotional book, *God is Faithful: A Daily Invitation into the Father Heart of God*, included a devotion entitled "Fear that Leads to Life":

"The prophets warn us that when we see God shaking the nations and perilous times come, our natural man will fear. Ezekiel asked, *'Can your heart endure, or can your hands remain strong, in the days when I shall deal with you?'* (Ezekiel 22:14).

"When God warned Noah of His coming judgments and told him to build an ark, Noah was *'moved with godly fear'* (Hebrews 11:7). Even bold, courageous David said, *'My flesh trembles for fear of You, and I am afraid of your judgments'* (Psalm 119:120). When the prophet Habakkuk saw disastrous days ahead, he cried out, *'When I heard, my body trembled; my lips quivered at the voice; rottenness entered my bones; and I trembled in myself, that I might rest in the day of trouble'* (Habakkuk 3:16).

"As you read these passages, note that the fear coming upon these godly men was not a fleshly fear, but a reverential awe of the Lord. They were not afraid of the enemy of their souls-but they did fear God's righteous judgments. You see, they understood the awesome power behind the approaching calamities. They did not fear the outcome of the storm, but rather God's holiness. Likewise today, any fear we experience must come from a holy reverence for the Lord, and never from a fleshly anxiety about our fate.

"God despises all sinful fear in us-the fear of losing material things and wealth, a change in our standard of living. All over the world, people are filled with this kind of fear as they see economies deteriorating. They are afraid of losing everything they have labored for.

"If you are a child of God, your heavenly Father will not endure such unbelief in you. It is because He has a higher purpose for you: *'The Lord of hosts, Him shall you hallow [honor]; let Him be your fear, and let Him be your dread [awe]'* (Isaiah 8:13).

"Let God be your fear and awe. That kind of fear leads not to death, but to life!"

Reasons for the Fear of the Lord

Do you want to know more about the Father and His promises? Psalm 25:14 tells us:

"The secret of the LORD is with those who fear Him, and He will show them His covenant."

The *Life in the Spirit Study Bible* by Zondervan has an article entitled, "The Fear of the Lord" which includes this paragraph:

"In keeping with the meaning of the fear of the Lord are the following reasons for fearing him.

"(1) We should fear him because of his authority as the Creator of all things and people (Ps 33:6-9; 96:4-5; Jonah 1:9). The fact that God's awesome authority and power continue to be exercised over the elements of creation and over the human race is sufficient cause for fearing him (Ex. 20:18-20; Eccl. 3:14; Jonah 1:11-16; Mark 4:39-41).

"(2) The holiness of God and his separation from and constant opposition to sin and unrighteousness should cause us to fear him (Rev. 15:4).

"(3) The universal judgment of God at the end of history should cause us to fear him who judges all injustice and inequity (Dt. 17:12-13; Is. 59:18-19; Mal. 3:5; Heb. 10:26-31). It is a solemn and holy truth of Scripture that on the day of final judgment every person will give an account to God for his or her actions and the stewardship of life (Eccl. 12:14; Rom. 14:10, 12; 2 Cor. 5:10; Rev. 20:12-13).

"(4) God has promised to bless and honor all those who fear him, 'Humility and the fear of the Lord bring wealth and honor and life' (Prov. 22:4). Other blessings promised include protection from death (Prov. 14:26-27), provisions for our daily needs (Ps. 34:9; 111:5), and a long life (Prov. 10:27). Those who fear the Lord know that 'it will go better with God-fearing men,' regardless of what happens to the world around them (Eccl. 8:12-13)."

A Crucial Summary of Life

Solomon, who was the wisest and richest man on earth at one time, had fallen away from his once true devotion to God, and in the midst of disappointment, frustration and depression he wrote the book of Ecclesiastes as a commentary on the meaninglessness of life without God. At the end of that book, he had this final, crucial summary:

"Now all has been heard; here is the conclusion of the matter: *Fear God and keep his commandments, for this is the whole [duty] of man*" (Ecclesiastes 12:13, emphasis mine).

Takeaway Highlight

What is the fear of the Lord? Fear of the Lord is having a deep awe, reverence, and respect for Him; and a healthy fear of doing anything that would displease Him. It is honoring God as God because of His great glory, holiness, majesty and power. It is the result of a deep appreciation of our own nothingness and of the infinite greatness and majesty of God. It stands opposed to pride and self-confidence.

For believers, it is not a fear that God will ever judge them for their sin (John 5:24; Romans 8:1). However, all God's children should possess a holy fear that trembles at the Word of God and causes them to turn away from evil.

Practical Application

Consider these questions: Am I more concerned with pleasing people, or with pleasing God? Am I fearful and anxious over worldly matters, or do I possess peace in the middle of the storm because I trust God with every circumstance and situation concerning me and the ones I love? Do I spend time daily in prayer and with God's Word humbly and gratefully communing with Him? Ask the Father to help you develop a healthy fear of the Lord.

Our reverent awe and respect for Jehovah God reflected in a proper fear of the Lord will motivate our Spirit-inspired desire to appreciate His love, worship His holiness, and praise His faithfulness. What does it mean to worship Him in Spirit and in truth? Let's see...

WORSHIP AND PRAISE

As we continue to grow in our relationship with God, our hearts will increasingly overflow with thankfulness, love, praise and worship. The Holy Spirit inflames our desire to spend time in the Presence of Jehovah, and we progressively recognize the fullness of all we have received through the sacrifice of our Lord Jesus Christ on the Cross. Our natural response is to worship and praise our Father God. He alone is worthy to be praised!

One of the most important ways we worship God is through our daily lives. In Romans 12:1, Paul said, "I appeal to you therefore, brothers, by the mercies of God, to present your bodies as a living sacrifice, holy and acceptable to God, which is your spiritual worship."

"We are created to worship through our lives. Every word, thought, action and emotion can be done as worship if we will seek to commune with God in everything. God never leaves us; he never

forsakes us (Deuteronomy 31:6). If we will keep our hearts open, we can live in the presence of our Creator, filled with the knowledge of his love and nearness in all we do." Craig Denison

Singing is not the only form of worship but it can be a very important element in honoring His presence when the Body of Christ assembles. Craig Denison is a worship leader in Dallas, TX. In his daily devotional entitled "What is Worship" (www.first15.org), he wrote:

"What is worship? When we go to church or gather with other believers why do we sing? Clearly not everyone finds singing or music to be their greatest passion, so why do we do it?

"Worship is first and foremost about the longing of God for unfettered relationship with his people. In authentic worship we can touch the heart of our Creator– satisfying the desires of he who paid the highest price simply to have us. Scripture is clear that God loves when we sing to him and about him. Ephesians 5:18-19 tells us to *'be filled with the Spirit, addressing one another in psalms and hymns and spiritual songs, singing and making melody to the Lord with your heart.'* John 4:23 states, *'But the hour is coming, and is now here, when the true worshipers will worship the Father in spirit and truth, for the Father is seeking such people to worship him.'*

"God loves worship. He longs for it. Think of that! You have an opportunity every day, through worship, to satisfy the heart of the one who paints sunsets, breathes life into dust and forms mountains, galaxies, animals, angels and humankind with just the power of his voice. You bring your Creator immense joy and satisfaction when you worship.

"You see, God is after your heart. He's after direct connection from his Spirit to yours. Music has this profound ability to reach past our limited understanding and help our heart connect with he who is limitless and eternal. It serves as an avenue for this cyclical, reciprocal act of love and devotion between the Creator and the created. In worship we discover the reality of God on a level different than reading Scripture or spending time in prayer or community. In worship we can sing to God songs of adoration, thanksgiving, high praise and unadulterated love in response to his character, nearness and devotion. Simply put, in worship we give and receive that which is most important– love.

"Whether engaging in personal worship is normal for you right now or not, know that you were created to worship. You were made to connect directly with the heart of God. As you engage in the act of worship you will discover the nearness of a God so filled with steadfast love and devotion for you that everything changes. As you consistently touch the heart of the Father your life will be transformed by his limitless grace and passionate pursuit. Engaging in worship will result in an overflowing, unquenchable joy as there is no greater experience than that of a perfect God meeting with imperfect man."

"Worship is our response to the overtures of love from the heart of the Father. Its central reality is found 'in Spirit and in Truth.' It is kindled within us only when then the Spirit of God touches our human Spirit. Forms and rituals do not produce worship, nor does the formal disuse

of forms and rituals. We can use all the right techniques and methods, we can have the best possible liturgy but we have not worshiped the Lord until Spirit touches Spirit. Singing, praying, praising, all may lead to worship, but worship is more than any of them. Our Spirit must be ignited by divine fire." Richard J. Foster, from his book, *Celebration of Discipline*

Every person on earth has been given the privilege to be able to worship and praise the Creator. While we are living we must take every opportunity to seek God's Presence and praise Him for His goodness.

Psalm 115:17-18 (NASB), says, *"The dead do not praise the LORD, nor do any who go down into silence; but as for us, we will bless the LORD from this time forth and forever. Praise the Lord!"* About this verse, Derek Prince wrote in a devotional entitled, "Who Should Praise the Lord":

"The Bible exhorts every area of creation and every kind of creature to praise the Lord. The Bible exhorts the heavens, the earth, the sea, the forests, the rocks – there is nothing that should not praise the Lord.

"It speaks about all kinds of creatures: flying creatures, creatures in the sea, crawling creatures, cattle, and wild beasts. It speaks about all the states of the human race: kings, princes, young men, old men, maidens, children – all are exhorted to praise the Lord. In fact, there is only just one category of people that do not praise the Lord. You know who that is? The dead. Only the dead do not praise the Lord.

"My dear friend, if you do not praise the Lord, you know what your problem is? You are one of the dead. Not necessarily physically dead, but spiritually dead. Come alive! Begin to praise the Lord. The more you praise the Lord, the more joy and spiritual life you will experience. Begin to praise Him right now."

Regarding the history of worship in the Bible, I found a research article entitled, "Worship," from the *Life in the Spirit Study Bible*, by Zondervan, in which the following paragraphs appear following their quotation of Nehemiah 8:5-6:

"Ezra opened the book. All the people could see him because he was standing above them; and as he opened it, the people all stood up. Ezra praised the Lord, the great God; and all the people lifted their hands and responded 'Amen! Amen!' Then they bowed down and worshiped the LORD with their faces to the ground."

"The English word 'worship' is derived from an Old English word 'worthship', and constitutes those actions and attitudes that ascribe honor and worth to the great God of heaven and earth. Worship is essentially God-centered, not human-centered. In Christian worship we draw near to God with joy and gratitude for what he has done for us in Christ and through the Holy Spirit. Worship expresses faith, love and devotion from our hearts and with our lives to God the Father and to the worthy lamb who was slain for our sins (cf. Revelation 4-5).

"Human beings have worshiped God from the beginning of history. Adam and Eve had fellowship regularly with God in the Garden of Eden (cf. Genesis 3:8). Cain and Abel both brought offerings (Heb. *minhah*, also translated as 'tribute' or 'gift') of plant life and animal life to God (Genesis 4:3-4); Seth's descendants called '*on the name of the Lord*' (Genesis 4:26). Noah built an altar to the Lord for a burnt offering after the flood (Genesis 8:20). Abraham dotted the landscape of the promised land with altars for burnt offerings to the Lord (Genesis 12:7-8; 13:4, 18; 22:9) and talked intimately with him (Genesis 18:23-33; 22:11-18).

"Not until after the exodus, when the tabernacle was built, however, did public worship become formalized. Thereafter, regular sacrifices were offered daily and especially on the Sabbath, and God established several annual holy feasts as occasions for Israel to commemorate their faith and to worship God corporately (Exodus 23:14-17; Leviticus 1-7; 16; 23:4-44; Deuteronomy 12; 16).This worship later became centralized around the temple in Jerusalem (cf. David's plans as recorded in 1 Chronicles 22-26). When the temple was destroyed in 586 B.C., the Jews built synagogues as places of instruction and worship while they were in exile and wherever they settled. These buildings continued to be used for worship even after the building of the second temple under Zerubbabel's leadership (Ezra 3-6). There were synagogues in Palestine and all over the Roman world during NT times (e.g. Luke 4:16; John 6:59; Acts 6:9; 13:14; 14:1; 17:1, 10; 18:4; 19:8; 22:19).

"Worship in the early church took place both in the Jerusalem temple and in private homes (Acts 2:46-47). Outside of Jerusalem, Christians worshiped, as long as they were permitted, in the synagogues; when that was no longer allowed, they met elsewhere for worship-usually in private homes (cf. Acts 18:7; Romans 16:5: Colossians 4:15; Philemon 2), though sometimes in public halls (Acts 19:9-10)."

The article continues, "when worship occurs from the heart in spirit and truth, God has many blessings in store for his people. He promises:

1. to be with them (Matthew 18:20) and to come into intimate communion (Revelation 3:20);

2. to overshadow his people with his glory (cf. Exodus 40:35; 2 Chronicles 7:1; 1 Peter 4:14);

3. to bless his people with showers of blessings (Ezekiel 34:26), especially with peace (Psalm 29:11);

4. to impart an abundance of joy (Psalm 122:1; John 15:11);

5. to answer the prayers of those who pray in sincere faith (Mark 11:24; James 5:15);

6. to freshly fill his people with his Holy Spirit and with boldness (Acts 4:31);

7. to send manifestations of the Holy Spirit among his people (1 Corinthians 12:7-13);

8. to guide his people into all truth through the Holy Spirit (John 15:26; 16:13);

9. to sanctify his people by his Word and his Spirit (John 17:17-19);

10. to comfort, encourage and strengthen his people (Isaiah 40:1; 1 Corinthians 14:26; 2 Corinthians 1:3-4; 1 Thessalonians 5:11);

11. to convict his people of sin, righteousness and judgment by the Holy Spirit (John 16:8); and,

12. to save sinners who become convicted of sin at a worship service (1 Corinthians 14:22-25)."

In a research article entitled "Praise," the *Life in the Spirit Study Bible*, by Zondervan, the question is asked, "Why do people praise the Lord?" They answer their own question with the following four reasons:

1. One of the obvious reasons is because of the splendor, glory, majesty and beauty of our God, the One who created the heavens and the earth (Psalms 96:4-6; 145:3; 148:13), the One who is to be exalted in his holiness (Psalm 99:3; Isaiah 6:3).

2. The experience of God's mighty acts, particularly his acts of salvation and redemption, is a key reason to praise his name (Psalms 96:1-3; 106:1-2; 148:14; 150:2; Luke 1:68-75; 2:14, 20); in doing so, we praise God for his unfailing mercy, grace and love (Psalms 57:9-10; 89:1-2; 117; 145:8-10; Ephesians 1:6).

3. We will also want to praise God for any specific acts of deliverance in our lives, such as being rescued from our enemies or healed of our sicknesses (Psalms 9:1-5; 40:1-3; 59:16; 124; Jeremiah 20:13; Luke 13:13; Acts 3:7-9)

4. Finally, our God's continual providential care and provision for us day by day, both physically and spiritually, is a powerful reason to praise and bless his name (Psalms 68:19; 103; 147; Isaiah 63:7).

Psalm 132:7 says, *"Let us go to his dwelling place; let us worship at his footstool!"*

Concerning this verse, Craig Denison wrote: "When we worship, we enter into direct contact with our all-powerful, all-loving, all-knowing heavenly Father. God's desire in worship is to draw us near to himself, fill us to overflow with his love, and wait patiently for us to love him in return. The more often we receive his love through worship, the more consistently we will love and honor him in all we do."

God will not make us worship Him or give Him praise. It is our free-will choice. If we choose to do so, it must be from a sincere, willing heart.

Along these lines, in a devotional entitled, "Choosing to Worship," Craig Denison wrote:

"When we choose to worship God here on earth, we are declaring to the Father and all of creation that he is King of kings and Lord of lords, and that he is our true ambition. To worship God here is to crown him as Lord of your life, come underneath his leadership, and make him first priority. What we do with our limited time here on earth has the power to affect the heart of God for all eternity. And living a lifestyle of worship instead of choosing the things of the world has the power to guide others into relationship with the Father, thereby changing the nature of their eternities forever."

Takeaway Highlight

As we continue to grow in our relationship with God, our hearts will increasingly overflow with thankfulness, love, praise and worship. The Holy Spirit inflames our desire to spend time in the Presence of

Jehovah, and we progressively recognize the fullness of all we have received through the sacrifice of our Lord Jesus Christ on the Cross. Our natural response is to worship and praise our Father God. He alone is worthy to be praised!

Practical Application

Think about the ways you personally worship and praise God. Is it only in Church one day a week? Or, maybe you have a daily time of fellowship and devotional quiet time alone with God during which you focus your love, admiration, and thankfulness towards Him. In what ways does your daily life bring Him honor and praise? Ask the Holy Spirit to help you worship God in spirit and in truth.

Worship and praise helps us know we can have an intimate relationship with God. It is almost unbelievable, but it's true. Not only that, He actually seeks, desires, and even longs for, a relationship with us! Let's consider more about this relationship...

RELATIONSHIP
WITH
OUR FATHER

Our greatest privilege and blessing is that we are able to have an intimate personal relationship with our Heavenly Father by and through His Holy Spirit. Jesus made it possible. Knowing more about Jesus helps us know the Father.

Jesus said, *"If you really know me, you will know my Father as well..."* John 14:7. If you want to know what the Father looks like, look at the Son: *"The Son is the image of the invisible God, the firstborn over all creation"* Colossians 1:15. Jesus also said, *"Anyone who has seen me has seen the Father"* John 14:9. Jesus enabled us to see the Father in a new way.

Derek Prince, in a devotional entitled "Relationship with Our Father," contained in *Declaring God's Word, A 365-day Devotional*, wrote:

"In the last two verses of John 17, we find the final utterance of Jesus to His disciples before He suffered and died on the cross. I believe that these two verses are the climax of the entire purpose of the gospel. Here is part of the prayer that Jesus prayed.

"O righteous Father! The world has not known You, but I have known You; and these [disciples] have known that You sent Me. And I have declared to them Your name... John 17:25-26a

"The name Jesus came to reveal was Father. You find very few uses of the word Father as a title of God in the Old Testament. The only person who could fully reveal the Father was the Son. Then, Jesus said,

"I have declared to them Your name, and will declare it, that the love with which You loved Me may be in them, and I in them. John 17:26

"The ultimate purpose of the gospel is this love relationship with God by which God loves us in exactly the same way that He loved–and still loves-Jesus, and that we love God in exactly the same way that Jesus loves Him. That is the purpose-to bring us into the family of God, to bring us into a relationship with God as Father that is the same relationship that Jesus has. It enables us to love God with the same love with which Jesus loves Him. You cannot ask for more. It is unimaginable. It is past our human minds to conceive what it entails. But it is the goal, the ultimate purpose. Everything else is secondary."

Brothers and sisters in Christ, let us strive to receive and give this kind of love in our pursuit of intimacy of relationship with our Heavenly Father!

Your Father Gives Good Gifts

One of my favorite daily devotionals is by Craig Denison, www.first15.org. In his devotional entitled "Your Father Gives Good Gifts" he wrote:

"One of my favorite parts of God's heart is his desire to give us amazing gifts. James 1:17 says, *'Every good gift and every perfect gift is from above, coming down from the Father of lights with whom there is no variation or shadow due to change.'* Every good gift you receive is because God loves you. His love for you is so great that he looks for every opportunity to give you a gift. He desperately wants you to know that you are loved and valued by him. He so deeply wants you to know that he is not distant from you but, rather, is working in your midst to lead you to abundant joy, peace and life.

"Matthew 7:11 says, *'If you then, who are evil, know how to give good gifts to your children, how much more will your Father who is in heaven give good things to those who ask him!'* I love how God has chosen to be known to us as a Father. And because God has chosen to reveal himself as a Father, we can more tangibly understand the love of God by looking to good earthly parents. God longs to bless you the way a good Father would. And at the same time, he loves you more deeply and powerfully than any earthly parent ever could. Our heavenly Father far outdoes any example an earthly father gives us. What gift are you longing for today? Do you long for friendship? Do you need a greater sense of being loved? Do you just need to know that he is with you?

"Thanking God for what he's already given us is a powerful way to position our hearts to be receptive to what he will give us in the future. Life is so much better when we acknowledge what God is doing in our midst. Knowing you are loved, liked and cared for is better than any material possession you could receive. You have a heavenly Father who gives amazing gifts. Celebrate his love today. And receive all that he longs to give you."

God our Father

In another devotional entitled "God our Father" on www.first15.org Craig Denison wrote:

"See what kind of love the Father has given to us, that we should be called children of God; and so we are." 1 John 3:1

"As a follower of Jesus you have been brought into the family of God. Take a moment to let that truth sink in. Think about what it means to have God, the Creator of the universe, the embodiment of Perfect Love, as your Father. So often we lose sight of the fact that God is our Father and view him through perspectives not aligned with Scripture. We view God through lenses the world and unfortunate experiences have given us rather than a revelation of him as a good Father given to us by the revolutionary teaching of Jesus.

"In Matthew 19:14, Jesus displays the heart of the Father when he says, *'Let the little children come to me and do not hinder them, for to such belongs the kingdom of heaven.'* As our Father, God longs for us as his children to simply be with him. He longs for us to know his love and embrace – to let it be the foundation of everything we do. More than God desires any task of you, he longs for your heart. So great was his desire for just the opportunity of relationship with you that Jesus displayed the fullness of God's unconditional love by willingly laying down his life for you. There is no room in Scripture to view God as anything but perfectly loving and good. View God as the good Father he is, and run to him with open arms and an open heart that you might find fullness of life in his eternal embrace.

"In every trial and circumstance you face today, God has a plan to lead you perfectly. He is not a God who sits back and watches as we try to figure life out. He wants to get involved in all that you do, just as a perfect Father wants to help his children succeed and live with joy. Ask God what he thinks about what you're doing. If you run into a problem today, ask for the Spirit's guidance. Doing your day with God is the absolute best way to live. He knows everything and has a perfect plan for you! Take time today to listen to God and trust his leading."

Seeing God as Father

First15.org devotionals are available free to your email inbox daily. I recommend you subscribe at your earliest opportunity. In another Craig Denison devotional entitled "Seeing God as Father," he wrote in part:

"Yet for us there is one God, the Father, from whom are all things and for whom we exist, and one Lord, Jesus Christ, through whom are all things and through whom we exist." 1 Corinthians 8:6

"If there's one name for God that has the power to dramatically transform the lives of believers, it's that we can call God 'Abba' or 'Father.' To see God as our Father changes everything. In Brennan Manning's book, *The Furious Longing of God*, he asks a pertinent and powerful question: 'Is your own personal prayer life characterized by the simplicity, childlike candor, boundless trust, and easy familiarity of a little one crawling up in Daddy's lap? An assured knowing that the daddy doesn't care if the child falls asleep, starts playing with toys, or even starts chatting with little friends, because the daddy knows the child has essentially chosen to be with him for that moment? Is that the spirit of your interior prayer life?'

"If we're going to center our lives around meeting with God, we must understand the nature of his love for us. We must begin to relate to him as our good and loving Father above all else. We must cast aside any notion that he is angry with us, far from us or void of affection or desire for us. We will only be drawn to our heavenly Father to the degree that we take him at his word and trust in his love for us. Take time today to receive the overwhelming, unconditional love of God for you. Allow his love to reorient your perspectives and beliefs. And respond to his great love by opening your heart and having fellowship with your Creator, Sustainer and all-loving heavenly Father."

Takeaway Highlight

"The ultimate purpose of the gospel is this love relationship with God by which God loves us in exactly the same way that He loved–and still loves-Jesus, and that we love God in exactly the same way that

Jesus loves Him. That is the purpose-to bring us into the family of God, to bring us into a relationship with God as Father that is the same relationship that Jesus has. It enables us to love God with the same love with which Jesus loves Him. You cannot ask for more. It is unimaginable. It is past our human minds to conceive what it entails. But it is the goal, the ultimate purpose. Everything else is secondary." Derek Prince

Practical Application

What can you do to begin to center your life around meeting with your Heavenly Father every day? He is worthy of our time and devotion. How do you think you can better pursue intimacy of relationship with Him?

A relationship with the Heavenly Father is not possible until you have been born again. That is the only way to be His child. Are you certain you are a child of God? Consider carefully...

ARE YOU
A CHILD OF
THE FATHER?

In order to have an ongoing, intimate relationship with Father God you must first be His child. Are you a child of God? Have you been born again? If you died today, are you certain you would go to heaven?

It is very common to hear someone say, "We are all God's children," and they mean all humans everywhere. Have you heard that? It is not true. We are all created by God, and loved by God, but we are not a child of God until we have been born again.

In John 3:3 Jesus said, *"Very truly I tell you, no one can see the kingdom of God unless they are born again."*

John writes this about Jesus, *"He came to that which was his own, but his own did not receive him. Yet to all who did receive him, to those who believed in his name, he gave the right to become children of God— children born not of natural descent, nor of human decision or a husband's will, but born of God."* John 1:11-13

"For God so loved the world that he gave his one and only Son, that whoever believes in him shall not perish but have eternal life." John 3:16

Jesus came to give us the right to become children of God if we repent of our sins, receive Him and the work He did on the Cross, and believe in His Name. Have you repented, believed and committed your life to Jesus?

Being the Child of God

Craig Denison, www.first15.org, has some great insight into what it means to be a child of God. In his devotional, "Being the Child of God" he wrote in part:

"And because you are sons, God has sent the Spirit of his Son into our hearts, crying, 'Abba! Father!' So you are no longer a slave, but a son, and if a son, then an heir through God." Galatians 4:6-7

"You are the child of God, brought into his family by the power and grace of Jesus' sacrifice for you. As believers, we hear we are God's children. But often we don't live our lives in response to that truth and instead live out of the mindset of an orphan. Children don't worry when they have a good father. They don't wonder if they'll be able to eat, if they're loved or if they have a place in this world. The unconditional love of a parent lays a foundation for them to have secure peace and joy. Your God desires the same for you. God wants to lay an unshakable foundation for you based solely on his love for you as his child so that when the storms come and waves crash over you, you remain strong in your identity.

"First, let's look at what Scripture says about you, and then take some time to respond to God's word in faith. John 1:12-13 says, *"But to all who did receive him, who believed in his name, he gave the right to become children of God, who were born, not of blood nor of the will of the flesh nor of the will of man, but of God."* Galatians 4:6-7 says, *"And because you are sons, God has sent the Spirit of his Son into our hearts, crying, 'Abba! Father!' So you are no longer a slave, but a son, and if a son, then an heir through God."* Finally, 2 Corinthians 6:18 says, *"And I will be a father to you, and you shall be sons and daughters to me, says the Lord Almighty."* Through adoption into God's family you are now a co-heir with Christ. Romans 8:17 says that we are God's children, *"and if children, then heirs—heirs of God and fellow heirs with Christ."* You were born again into God's family when you asked Jesus to be your Lord and Saviour.

"So what does it mean to be God's child? What does it mean to be a co-heir with Christ? It means that all that is God's is yours. He shares with you his Kingdom. You have a Father who gives you amazing gifts. You have a Father who absolutely loves spending time with you. Your heavenly Dad's love for you knows no bounds. His love is pervasive, powerful and freely given. You no longer need to worry about whether you have a place in this world. There's no need to concern yourself with whether you will have clothes or food. You no longer have to live in pursuit of the opinions of those around you. God enjoys you. He has a plan for you. He doesn't take being your Father lightly. He takes complete ownership of his responsibility. He will strengthen you, teach you, develop you and give you a life of passion and meaning. To be the child of God is to be loved, liked and completely cared for.

"So how can you live in response to God's word? How can you get out of the mindset of an orphan? You must have faith that God is who he says he is and believe he will do what he's promised to do. Romans 10:17 says that *"faith comes from hearing, and hearing through the word of Christ."* You have heard the word of the Lord today. You are his child. He promises to provide for you. So have faith! Faith isn't something you just conjure up. It's a response to God's faithfulness. God has and will be faithful to you. Allow his word to stir up faith within you today. Live in response to his promises and allow the peace and joy of being God's child to lay an unshakable foundation for you today.

"*'And I will be a father to you, and you shall be sons and daughters to me, says the Lord Almighty.'* 2 Corinthians 6:18

"God's love for you is sure. There is nothing you could ever do to remove yourself from his family. Once you are his child, you are his forever. As a Christian you are living under God's grace, not works. God loves you because he loves you– not because of what you think about yourself or what you do. Therefore, release any thoughts you have of yourself that don't line up with God's word. Let go of any burdens you're carrying today in light of his love. And experience the transforming power of a life lived in response to the faithfulness of God."

Takeaway Highlight

"So what does it mean to be God's child? What does it mean to be a co-heir with Christ? It means that all that is God's is yours. He shares with you his Kingdom. You have a Father who gives you amazing gifts. You have a Father who absolutely loves spending time with

you. Your heavenly Dad's love for you knows no bounds. His love is pervasive, powerful and freely given. You no longer need to worry about whether you have a place in this world. There's no need to concern yourself with whether you will have clothes or food. You no longer have to live in pursuit of the opinions of those around you. God enjoys you. He has a plan for you. He doesn't take being your Father lightly. He takes complete ownership of his responsibility. He will strengthen you, teach you, develop you and give you a life of passion and meaning. To be the child of God is to be loved, liked and completely cared for." Craig Denison

Practical Application

Consider this prayer transcribed from a sermon by Derek Prince: "God, I thank you that you are my Father, and that I am your child. You really love me. I am not rejected. I am not unwanted. I am a member of the family of God — the best family in the universe. Thank you, God. You are my Father. I am your child. You love me and I love you! Thank you, thank you, thank you, God. In Jesus' name. Amen"

Have you given your heart to Jesus? If not, and you would like to do so now, there is additional guidance on page 107.

Let us all renew our commitment to pursue intimacy of relationship with God our Father. What an amazing Father He is!

TAKE ACTION

You Can Have "The Real Thing"

"The Real Thing" has nothing to do with "religion." Rather, it is an intimate personal relationship with our Heavenly Father, because of the finished work of Jesus at the Cross. The Holy Spirit comes and seals us as His very own, and begins an ongoing work in us to conform us to the image of Christ Jesus.

You can begin this exciting and abundant life today. It will continue throughout all eternity.

First, acknowledge and confess that you have sinned against God.

Second, renounce your sins – determine that you are not going back to them. Turn away from sin. Turn to God.

Third, by faith receive Christ into your heart. Surrender your life completely to Him. He will come to live in your heart by the Holy Spirit.

You can do this right now.

Start by simply talking to God. You can pray a prayer like this:

"Oh God, I am a sinner. I'm sorry for my sin. I want to turn from my sin. Please forgive me. I believe Jesus Christ is Your Son; I believe He died on the Cross for my sin and You raised Him to life. I want to trust Him as my Savior and follow Him as my Lord from this day forward, forevermore. Lord Jesus, I put my trust in You and surrender my life to You. Please come into my life and fill me with your Holy Spirit. In Jesus' Name Amen."

If you just said this prayer, and you meant it with all your heart, we believe you just got Saved and are now Born Again in Christ Jesus as a totally new person.

"Therefore, if anyone is in Christ, he is a new creation; the old has gone, the new has come!" (II Corinthians 5:17)

We urge you to go "all in and all out for the All in All"! (Pastor Mark Batterson, *All In*)

We suggest you follow the Lord in water baptism at your earliest opportunity. Water baptism is an outward symbol of the inward change that follows your salvation and re-birth.

The grace of God Himself gives you the desire and ability to surrender completely to the Holy Spirit's work in and through you (Philippians 2:13).

The Baptism in the Holy Spirit is His empowerment for you.

You Can Receive the Baptism
in the Holy Spirit

The Baptism in the Holy Spirit is a separate experience and a Holy privilege granted to those who ask. This is God's own power to enable you to live an abundant, overcoming life. The Bible says it is the same power that raised Jesus from the dead (Romans 1:4; 8:11; ll Cor. 4:13-14; 1 Peter 3:18).

Have you asked the Father for Jesus to baptize you (immerse you) in the Holy Spirit (Luke 3:16)? If you ask the Father, He will give Him to you (Luke 11:13). Have you allowed the "rivers of living water" to flow from within you (John 7:38-39)? Our Father desires for us to walk in all His fullness by His Holy Spirit.

The power to witness, and live your life the way Jesus did in intimate relationship with the Father, comes from asking Jesus to baptize you in the Holy Spirit. To receive this baptism, pray along these lines:

Abba Father and my Lord Jesus,

Thank you for giving me your Spirit to live inside me. I am saved by grace through faith in Jesus. I ask you now to baptize me in the Holy Ghost with Your fire and power. I fully receive it through faith just like I did my salvation. Now, Holy Spirit, come and rise up within me as I praise God! Fill me up Jesus!

I fully expect to receive my prayer language as You give me utterance. In Jesus' Name. Amen.

Now, out loud, begin to praise and glorify JESUS, because He is the baptizer of the Holy Spirit! From deep in your spirit, tell Him, "I love you, I thank you, I praise you, Jesus."

Repeat this as you feel joy and gratefulness bubble up from deep inside you. Speak those words and syllables you receive – not in your own language, but the heavenly language given to you by the Holy Spirit. Allow this joy to come out of you in syllables of a language your own mind does not already know. That will be your prayer language the Spirit will use through you when you don't know how to pray (Romans 8:26-28). It is not the "gift of tongues" for public use, therefore it does not require a public interpretation.

You have to surrender and use your own vocal chords to verbally express your new prayer language. The Holy Spirit is a gentleman. He will not force you to speak. Don't be concerned with how it sounds. It is a heavenly language!

Worship Him! Praise Him! Use your heavenly language by praying in the Spirit every day! Paul urges us to "pray in the Spirit on all occasions with all kinds of prayers and requests." (Ephesians 6:18)

Your heavenly language of tongues for prayer might not come immediately. It is only one evidence of the Baptism in the Holy Spirit. Some others are: a hunger for the Word of God; a thirst for righteousness; a desire for sanctification and a daily surrender to the leading of the Holy Spirit.

Draw near to God daily. He will draw near to you (James 4:8).

Contact Us

We would love to hear your feedback or answer your questions.

- We would especially like to know if you made a decision to receive Jesus into your heart and prayed the prayer of Salvation on page 108. Or maybe you had prayed a similar prayer before, but this is the first time you really meant it from your heart. Tell us about your decision.

- Perhaps you made a decision to rededicate your life to Christ – to go "all in and all out" for Jesus! If so, we would like to know so we can encourage you. Please write to us.

- If you prayed the prayer to ask Jesus to baptize you in the Holy Spirit, please tell us.

As a further aid and encouragement, we would like to teach you more about how to follow Jesus – how to be a true disciple. A disciple is a "disciplined learner" and we want to share many truths with you about how to have an intimate relationship with God the Father, by the Holy Spirit. Jesus came to reconcile us to the Father. We want to help you develop a meaningful relationship with Him.

Please ask us to include you in our Discipleship Program whereby you will receive an encouraging teaching every three months or so. This is not the kind of lesson you are required to fill in and send back to us. You must only desire to be encouraged regularly in the Lord, and be willing to prayerfully study the materials. That's all.

Please send your comments, questions and feedback to:

Freedom in Jesus Prison Ministries
Attn: Stephen – KTF
P.O. Box 939
Levelland, TX 79336

Ask your loved ones to check out our ministry website at *www.fijm.org.*

They can learn more about Stephen Canup's books at *www.stephencanup.com.*

We pray you are blessed abundantly by our Father every day, in every way, in Christ Jesus as you seek Him daily in and by the Holy Spirit!

I Challenge You!!!

God is able to transform your life in the same way He did mine. Understanding and receiving God's love is key; and, willing obedience is necessary.

But you must understand that He rewards those who diligently and earnestly seek Him (Hebrews 11:6); and, that you are transformed by renewing your mind through applying the principles in His Word to your daily life (Romans 12:1-2).

I challenge you to:

- Start every day with the Word and the Spirit. Ask the Holy Spirit to help you apply His Truth to your life. Let the Spirit use the Word to transform you.

- Look up every scripture reference in this book. Mark the verses in your own Bible. Memorize the ones that mean the most to you.

- Study the scriptural principles in this book in small groups. Sharing concepts from the Word with others helps you learn and apply them to your life.

- Show this book to others. As an ambassador for Christ (see 2 Corinthians 5:18-20), please use this book as a tool to reach the lost and encourage the Body of Believers. After sharing it with them, encourage them then to contact me to request their own copy of the book so they can study it and loan it to others. Each person who wants one must write me individually because I can only send one book to each person.

- Pray daily for us and for our ministry. We need your prayers.

- Do you want to help us continue to provide books like these free to prisoners? At your first opportunity, begin a program of regular giving to us so we can better minister to others who want to be free from every form of bondage. Former prisoners helping prisoners is what we are all about.

FURTHER
REVIEW AND
APPLICATION

Holy Scriptures Referencing God as "Father"

The Scriptures verses and passages which follow were summarized and categorized by me in two earlier chapters entitled "Old Testament References to God as Father," and, "New Testament References to God as Father." **They represent every scripture in the Bible where I found the word "Father" ascribed to God.**

I challenge you to read them carefully and perhaps even re-categorize them. You may find more actions or attributes of the Father than I have already presented in the two aforementioned chapters.

Old Testament (emphasis added):

Deuteronomy 32:6 "Is this the way you repay the LORD, you foolish and unwise people? Is he not your **Father**, your Creator, who made you and formed you?"

Isaiah 9:6 "For to us a child is born, to us a son is given, and the government will be on his shoulders. And he will be called Wonderful Counselor, Mighty God, Everlasting **Father**, Prince of Peace."

Isaiah 63:16 "But you are our **Father**, though Abraham does not know us or Israel acknowledge us; you, LORD, are our **Father**, our Redeemer from of old is your name."

Isaiah 64:8 "Yet you, LORD, are our **Father**. We are the clay, you are the potter; we are all the work of your hand."

Jeremiah 3:4 "Have you not just called to me: 'My **Father**, my friend from my youth...'"

Jeremiah 3:19 "I myself said, 'How gladly would I treat you like my children and give you a pleasant land, the most beautiful inheritance of any nation.' I thought you would call me '**Father**' and not turn away from following me."

Malachi 2:10 "Do we not all have one **Father**? Did not one God create us? Why do we profane the covenant of our ancestors by being unfaithful to one another?"

New Testament (emphasis added):

Matthew 5:16 "In the same way, let your light shine before others, that they may see your good deeds and glorify your **Father** in heaven."

Matthew 5:45 "...that you may be children of your **Father** in heaven. He causes his sun to rise on the evil and the good, and sends rain on the righteous and the unrighteous."

Matthew 5:48 "Be perfect, therefore, as your heavenly **Father** is perfect."

Matthew 6:1 "Be careful not to practice your righteousness in front of others to be seen by them. If you do, you will have no reward from your **Father** in heaven."

Matthew 6:4 "...so that your giving may be in secret. Then your **Father**, who sees what is done in secret, will reward you."

Matthew 6:6 "But when you pray, go into your room, close the door and pray to your **Father**, who is unseen. Then your **Father**, who sees what is done in secret, will reward you."

Matthew 6:8-9 "Do not be like them, for your **Father** knows what you need before you ask him. 'This, then, is how you should pray: Our **Father** in heaven, hallowed be your name...'"

Matthew 6:14-15 "For if you forgive other people when they sin against you, your heavenly **Father** will also forgive you. But if you do not forgive others their sins, your **Father** will not forgive your sins."

Matthew 6:18 "...so that it will not be obvious to others that you are fasting, but only to your **Father**, who is unseen; and your **Father**, who sees what is done in secret, will reward you."

Matthew 6:26 "Look at the birds of the air; they do not sow or reap or store away in barns, and yet your heavenly **Father** feeds them. Are you not much more valuable than they?"

Matthew 6:32 "For the pagans run after all these things, and your heavenly **Father** knows that you need them."

Matthew 7:11 "If you, then, though you are evil, know how to give good gifts to your children, how much more will your Father in heaven give good gifts to those who ask him!"

Matthew 7:21 "Not everyone who says to me, 'Lord, Lord,' will enter the kingdom of heaven, but only the one who does the will of my **Father** who is in heaven."

Matthew 10:20 "...for it will not be you speaking, but the Spirit of your **Father** speaking through you."

Matthew 10:29 "Are not two sparrows sold for a penny? Yet not one of them will fall to the ground outside your **Father**'s care."

Matthew 10:32-33 "Whoever acknowledges me before others, I will also acknowledge before my **Father** in heaven. But whoever disowns me before others, I will disown before my **Father** in heaven."

Matthew 11:25-26 "At that time Jesus said, 'I praise you, **Father**, Lord of heaven and earth, because you have hidden these things from the wise and learned, and revealed them to little children. Yes, **Father**, for this is what you were pleased to do.'"

Matthew 11:27 "All things have been committed to me by my **Father**. No one knows the Son except the **Father**, and no one knows the **Father** except the Son and those to whom the Son chooses to reveal him."

Matthew 12:50 "For whoever does the will of my **Father** in heaven is my brother and sister and mother."

Matthew 13:43 "Then the righteous will shine like the sun in the kingdom of their **Father**. Whoever has ears, let them hear..."

Matthew 15:13 "He replied, 'Every plant that my heavenly **Father** has not planted will be pulled up by the roots.'"

Matthew 16:17 "Jesus replied, 'Blessed are you, Simon son of Jonah, for this was not revealed to you by flesh and blood, but by my **Father** in heaven.'"

Matthew 16:27 "For the Son of Man is going to come in his **Father**'s glory with his angels, and then he will reward each person according to what they have done."

Matthew 18:10 "See that you do not despise one of these little ones. For I tell you that their angels in heaven always see the face of my **Father** in heaven."

Matthew 18:14 "In the same way your **Father** in heaven is not willing that any of these little ones should perish."

Matthew 18:19 "Again, truly I tell you that if two of you on earth agree about anything they ask for, it will be done for them by my **Father** in heaven."

Matthew 18:35 "This is how my heavenly **Father** will treat each of you unless you forgive your brother or sister from your heart."

Matthew 20:23 "Jesus said to them, 'You will indeed drink from my cup, but to sit at my right or left is not for me to grant. These places belong to those for whom they have been prepared by my **Father**'"

Matthew 23:9 "And do not call anyone on earth 'father,' for you have one **Father**, and he is in heaven."

Matthew 24:36 "But about that day or hour no one knows, not even the angels in heaven, nor the Son, but only the **Father**."

Matthew 25:34 "Then the King will say to those on his right, 'Come, you who are blessed by my **Father**; take your inheritance, the kingdom prepared for you since the creation of the world.'"

Matthew 26:29 "I tell you, I will not drink from this fruit of the vine from now on until that day when I drink it new with you in my **Father**'s kingdom."

Matthew 26:39 "Going a little farther, he fell with his face to the ground and prayed, 'My **Father**, if it is possible, may this cup be taken from me. Yet not as I will, but as you will.'"

Matthew 26:42 "He went away a second time and prayed, 'My **Father**, if it is not possible for this cup to be taken away unless I drink it, may your will be done.'"

Matthew 26:53 "Do you think I cannot call on my **Father**, and he will at once put at my disposal more than twelve legions of angels?"

Matthew 28:19 Therefore go and make disciples of all nations, baptizing them in the name of the **Father** and of the Son and of the Holy Spirit,

Mark 8:38 "If anyone is ashamed of me and my words in this adulterous and sinful generation, the Son of Man will be ashamed of them when he comes in his **Father's** glory with the holy angels."

Mark 11:25 "And when you stand praying, if you hold anything against anyone, forgive them, so that your **Father** in heaven may forgive you your sins."

Mark 13:32 "But about that day or hour no one knows, not even the angels in heaven, nor the Son, but only the **Father**."

Mark 14:36 "Abba, **Father**, everything is possible for you. Take this cup from me. Yet not what I will, but what you will."

Luke 2:49 "Why were you searching for me?" he asked. "Didn't you know I had to be in my **Father's** house?"

Luke 6:36 "Be merciful, just as your **Father** is merciful."

Luke 9:26 "Whoever is ashamed of me and my words, the Son of Man will be ashamed of them when he comes in his glory and in the glory of the **Father** and of the holy angels."

Luke 10:21-22 "At that time Jesus, full of joy through the Holy Spirit, said, 'I praise you, **Father**, Lord of heaven and earth, because you have hidden these things from the wise and learned, and revealed them to little children. Yes, **Father**, for this is what you were pleased to do. All things have been committed to me by my **Father**. No one knows who the Son is except the **Father**, and no one knows who the **Father** is except the Son and those to whom the Son chooses to reveal him.'"

Luke 11:2 "He said to them, 'When you pray, say: **Father**, hallowed be your name, your kingdom come.'"

Luke 11:13 "If you then, though you are evil, know how to give good gifts to your children, how much more will your **Father** in heaven give the Holy Spirit to those who ask him!"

Luke 12:30 "For the pagan world runs after all such things, and your **Father** knows that you need them."

Luke 12:32 "Do not be afraid, little flock, for your **Father** has been pleased to give you the kingdom."

Luke 22:29 "And I confer on you a kingdom, just as my **Father** conferred one on me…"

Luke 22:42 "**Father**, if you are willing, take this cup from me; yet not my will, but yours be done."

Luke 23:34 "Jesus said, '**Father**, forgive them, for they do not know what they are doing.' And they divided up his clothes by casting lots."

Luke 23:46 "Jesus called out with a loud voice, '**Father**, into your hands 1 commit my spirit.' When he had said this, he breathed his last."

Luke 24:49 "1 am going to send you what my **Father** has promised; but stay in the city until you have been clothed with power from on high."

John 1:14 "The Word became flesh and made his dwelling among us. We have seen his glory, the glory of the one and only Son, who came from the **Father**, full of grace and truth."

John 1:18 "No one has ever seen God, but the one and only Son, who is himself God and is in closest relationship with the **Father,** has made him known."

John 2:16 "To those who sold doves he said, 'Get these out of here! Stop turning my **Father**'s house into a market!'"

John 3:35 "The **Father** loves the Son and has placed everything in his hands."

John 4:21 "Woman," Jesus replied, "believe me, a time is coming when you will worship the **Father** neither on this mountain nor in Jerusalem."

John 4:23 "Yet a time is coming and has now come when the true worshipers will worship the **Father** in the Spirit and in truth, for they are the kind of worshipers the **Father** seeks."

John 5:17-23 "In his defense Jesus said to them, 'My **Father** is always at his work to this very day, and I too am working.' For this reason they tried all the more to kill him; not only was he breaking the Sabbath, but he was even calling God his own **Father**, making himself equal with God. Jesus gave them this answer: 'Very truly I tell you, the Son can do nothing by himself; he can do only what he sees his **Father** doing, because whatever the **Father** does the Son also does. For the **Father** loves the Son and shows him all he does. Yes, and he will show him even greater works than these, so that you will be amazed. For just as the **Father** raises the dead and gives them life, even so the Son gives life to whom he is pleased to give it. Moreover, the **Father** judges no one, but has entrusted all judgment to the Son, that all may honor the Son just as they honor the **Father**. Whoever does not honor the Son does not honor the **Father**, who sent him.'"

John 5:26 "For as the **Father** has life in himself, so he has granted the Son also to have life in himself."

John 5:36-37 "I have testimony weightier than that of John. For the works that the **Father** has given me to finish—the very works that I am doing—testify that the **Father** has sent me. And the **Father** who sent me has himself testified concerning me. You have never heard his voice nor seen his form..."

John 5:43 "I have come in my **Father**'s name, and you do not accept me; but if someone else comes in his own name, you will accept him."

John 5:45 "But do not think I will accuse you before the **Father**. Your accuser is Moses, on whom your hopes are set."

John 6:27 "Do not work for food that spoils, but for food that endures to eternal life, which the Son of Man will give you. For on him God the **Father** has placed his seal of approval."

John 6:32 "Jesus said to them, 'Very truly I tell you, it is not Moses who has given you the bread from heaven, but it is my **Father** who gives you the true bread from heaven.'"

John 6:37 "All those the **Father** gives me will come to me, and whoever comes to me I will never drive away."

John 6:40 "For my **Father**'s will is that everyone who looks to the Son and believes in him shall have eternal life, and I will raise them up at the last day."

John 6:44-46 "No one can come to me unless the **Father** who sent me draws them, and I will raise them up at the last day. It is written in the Prophets: 'They will all be taught by God.' Everyone who has heard the **Father** and learned from him comes to me. No one has seen the **Father** except the one who is from God; only he has seen the **Father**."

John 6:57 "Just as the living **Father** sent me and I live because of the **Father**, so the one who feeds on me will live because of me."

John 6:65 "He went on to say, 'This is why I told you that no one can come to me unless the **Father** has enabled them.'"

John 8:16 "But if I do judge, my decisions are true, because I am not alone. I stand with the **Father**, who sent me."

John 8:18-19 "I am one who testifies for myself; my other witness is the **Father**, who sent me." Then they asked him, 'Where is your father?' 'You do not know me or my **Father**,' Jesus replied. 'If you knew me, you would know my **Father** also.'"

John 8:27-28 "They did not understand that he was telling them about his **Father**. So Jesus said, 'When you have lifted up the Son of Man, then you will know that I am he and that I do nothing on my own but speak just what the **Father** has taught me.'"

John 8:38 "I am telling you what I have seen in the **Father**'s presence, and you are doing what you have heard from your father."

John 8:41-42 "You are doing the works of your own father." 'We are not illegitimate children,' they protested. 'The only **Father** we have is God himself.' Jesus said to them, 'If God were your **Father**, you would love me, for I have come here from God. I have not come on my own; God sent me.'"

John 8:49 "I am not possessed by a demon," said Jesus, 'but I honor my **Father** and you dishonor me.'"

John 8:54 "Jesus replied, 'If I glorify myself, my glory means nothing. My **Father**, whom you claim as your God, is the one who glorifies me.'"

John 10:15"... just as the **Father** knows me and I know the **Father**—and I lay down my life for the sheep."

John 10:17-18 "The reason my **Father** loves me is that I lay down my life—only to take it up again. No one takes it from me, but I lay it down of my own accord. I have authority to lay it down and authority to take it up again. This command I received from my **Father**."

John 10:25 "Jesus answered, 'I did tell you, but you do not believe. The works I do in my **Father**'s name testify about me...'"

John 10:29-30 "My **Father**, who has given them to me, is greater than all; no one can snatch them out of my **Father**'s hand. I and the **Father** are one."

John 10:32 "...but Jesus said to them, 'I have shown you many good works from the **Father**. For which of these do you stone me?'"

John 10:36-38 "...what about the one whom the **Father** set apart as his very own and sent into the world? Why then do you accuse me of blasphemy because I said, 'I am God's Son'? Do not believe me unless I do the works of my **Father**. But if I do them, even though you do not believe me, believe the works, that you may know and understand that the **Father** is in me, and I in the **Father**."

John 11:41 "So they took away the stone. Then Jesus looked up and said, '**Father**, I thank you that you have heard me.'"

John 12:26-28 "Whoever serves me must follow me; and where I am, my servant also will be. My **Father** will honor the one who serves me. Now my soul is troubled, and what shall I say? '**Father**, save me from this hour'? No, it was for this very reason I came to this hour. **Father**, glorify your name! Then a voice came from heaven, 'I have glorified it, and will glorify it again.'"

John 12:49-50 "For I did not speak on my own, but the **Father** who sent me commanded me to say all that I have spoken. I know that his command leads to eternal life. So whatever I say is just what the **Father** has told me to say."

John 13:1 "It was just before the Passover Festival. Jesus knew that the hour had come for him to leave this world and go to the **Father**. Having loved his own who were in the world, he loved them to the end."

John 13:3 "Jesus knew that the **Father** had put all things under his power, and that he had come from God and was returning to God..."

John 14:2 "My **Father**'s house has many rooms; if that were not so, would I have told you that I am going there to prepare a place for you?"

John 14:6-13 "Jesus answered, 'I am the way and the truth and the life. No one comes to the **Father** except through me. If you really know me, you will know my **Father** as well. From now on, you do know him and have seen him.' Philip said, 'Lord, show us the **Father** and that will be enough for us.' Jesus answered: 'Don't you know me, Philip, even after I have been among you such a long time? Anyone who has seen me has seen the **Father**. How can you say, 'Show us the **Father**'? Don't you believe that I am in the **Father**, and that the **Father** is in me? The words I say to you I do not speak on my own authority. Rather, it is the **Father**, living in me, who is doing his work. Believe me when I say that I am in the **Father** and the **Father** is in me; or at least believe on the evidence of the works themselves. Very truly I tell you, whoever believes in me will do the works I have been doing, and they will do even greater things than these, because

I am going to the **Father**. And I will do whatever you ask in my name, so that the **Father** may be glorified in the Son.'"

John 14:16 "And I will ask the **Father**, and he will give you another advocate to help you and be with you forever—..."

John 14:20-21 "On that day you will realize that I am in my **Father**, and you are in me, and I am in you. Whoever has my commands and keeps them is the one who loves me. The one who loves me will be loved by my **Father**, and I too will love them and show myself to them."

John 14:23-24 "Jesus replied, 'Anyone who loves me will obey my teaching. My **Father** will love them, and we will come to them and make our home with them. Anyone who does not love me will not obey my teaching. These words you hear are not my own; they belong to the **Father** who sent me.'"

John 14:26 "But the Advocate, the Holy Spirit, whom the **Father** will send in my name, will teach you all things and will remind you of everything I have said to you."

John 14:28 "You heard me say, 'I am going away and I am coming back to you.' If you loved me, you would be glad that I am going to the **Father**, for the **Father** is greater than I."

John 14:31 "...but he comes so that the world may learn that I love the **Father** and do exactly what my **Father** has commanded me. Come now; let us leave."

John 15:1 "I am the true vine, and my **Father** is the gardener."

John 15:8-10 "This is to my **Father**'s glory, that you bear much fruit, showing yourselves to be my disciples. As the **Father** has loved me, so have I loved you. Now remain in my love. If you keep my commands, you will remain in my love, just as I have kept my **Father**'s commands and remain in his love."

John 15:15-16 "I no longer call you servants, because a servant does not know his master's business. Instead, I have called you friends, for everything that I learned from my **Father** I have made known to you. You did not choose me, but I chose you and appointed you so that you might go and bear fruit—fruit that will last—and so that whatever you ask in my name the **Father** will give you."

John 15:23-24 "Whoever hates me hates my **Father** as well. If I had not done among them the works no one else did, they would not be guilty of sin. As it is, they have seen, and yet they have hated both me and my **Father**."

John 15:26 "When the Advocate comes, whom I will send to you from the **Father**—the Spirit of truth who goes out from the **Father**—he will testify about me."

John 16:3 "They will do such things because they have not known the **Father** or me."

John 16:10 "...about righteousness, because I am going to the **Father**, where you can see me no longer..."

John 16:15 "All that belongs to the **Father** is mine. That is why I said the Spirit will receive from me what he will make known to you."

John 16:17 "At this, some of his disciples said to one another, 'What does he mean by saying, 'In a little while you will see me no more, and then after a little while you will see me,' and 'Because I am going to the **Father**'?"

John 16:23 "In that day you will no longer ask me anything. Very truly I tell you, my **Father** will give you whatever you ask in my name."

John 16:25-28 "Though I have been speaking figuratively, a time is coming when I will no longer use this kind of language but will tell you plainly about my **Father**. In that day you will ask in my name. I am not saying that I will ask the **Father** on your behalf. No, the **Father** himself loves you because you have loved me and have believed that I came from God. I came from the **Father** and entered the world; now I am leaving the world and going back to the **Father**."

John 16:32 "A time is coming and in fact has come when you will be scattered, each to your own home. You will leave me all alone. Yet I am not alone, for my **Father** is with me."

John 17:1 "After Jesus said this, he looked toward heaven and prayed: '**Father**, the hour has come. Glorify your Son, that your Son may glorify you.'"

John 17:5 "And now, **Father**, glorify me in your presence with the glory I had with you before the world began."

John 17:11 "I will remain in the world no longer, but they are still in the world, and I am coming to you. Holy **Father**, protect them by the power of your name, the name you gave me, so that they may be one as we are one."

John 17:21 "...that all of them may be one, **Father**, just as you are in me and I am in you. May they also be in us so that the world may believe that you have sent me."

John 17:24-25 "**Father**, I want those you have given me to be with me where I am, and to see my glory, the glory you have given me because you loved me before the creation of the world. Righteous **Father**, though the world does not know you, I know you, and they know that you have sent me."

John 18:11 "Jesus commanded Peter, 'Put your sword away! Shall I not drink the cup the **Father** has given me?'"

John 20:17 "Jesus said, 'Do not hold on to me, for I have not yet ascended to the **Father**. Go instead to my brothers and tell them, I am ascending to my **Father** and your **Father**, to my God and your God.'"

John 20:21 "Again Jesus said, 'Peace be with you! As the **Father** has sent me, I am sending you.'"

Acts 1:4 "On one occasion, while he was eating with them, he gave them this command: 'Do not leave Jerusalem, but wait for the gift my **Father** promised, which you have heard me speak about.'"

Acts 1:7 "He said to them: 'It is not for you to know the times or dates the **Father** has set by his own authority.'"

Acts 2:33 "Exalted to the right hand of God, he has received from the **Father** the promised Holy Spirit and has poured out what you now see and hear."

Romans 1:7 "To all in Rome who are loved by God and called to be his holy people: Grace and peace to you from God our **Father** and from the Lord Jesus Christ."

Romans 6:4 "We were therefore buried with him through baptism into death in order that, just as Christ was raised from the dead through the glory of the **Father**, we too may live a new life."

Romans 8:15 "The Spirit you received does not make you slaves, so that you live in fear again; rather, the Spirit you received brought about your adoption to sonship. And by him we cry, 'Abba, **Father**.'"

Romans 15:6 '...so that with one mind and one voice you may glorify the God and **Father** of our Lord Jesus Christ."

1 Corinthians 1:3 "Grace and peace to you from God our **Father** and the Lord Jesus Christ."

1 Corinthians 8:6 "...yet for us there is but one God, the **Father**, from whom all things came and for whom we live; and there is but one Lord, Jesus Christ, through whom all things came and through whom we live."

1 Corinthians 15:24 "Then the end will come, when he hands over the kingdom to God the **Father** after he has destroyed all dominion, authority and power."

2 Corinthians 1:2-3 "Grace and peace to you from God our **Father** and the Lord Jesus Christ. Praise be to the God and **Father** of our Lord Jesus Christ, the **Father** of compassion and the God of all comfort..."

2 Corinthians 6:18 "And, 'I will be a **Father** to you, and you will be my sons and daughters, says the Lord Almighty.'"

2 Corinthians 11:31 "The God and **Father** of the Lord Jesus, who is to be praised forever, knows that I am not lying."

Galatians 1:1 "Paul, an apostle—sent not from men nor by a man, but by Jesus Christ and God the **Father**, who raised him from the dead—..."

Galatians 1:3-4 "Grace and peace to you from God our **Father** and the Lord Jesus Christ, who gave himself for our sins to rescue us from the present evil age, according to the will of our God and **Father**..."

Galatians 4:6 "Because you are his sons, God sent the Spirit of his Son into our hearts, the Spirit who calls out, 'Abba, **Father**.'"

Ephesians 1:2-3 "Grace and peace to you from God our **Father** and the Lord Jesus Christ. Praise be to the God and **Father** of our Lord Jesus Christ, who has blessed us in the heavenly realms with every spiritual blessing in Christ."

Ephesians 1:17 "I keep asking that the God of our Lord Jesus Christ, the glorious **Father**, may give you the Spirit of wisdom and revelation, so that you may know him better."

Ephesians 2:18 "For through him we both have access to the **Father** by one Spirit."

Ephesians 3:14 "For this reason I kneel before the **Father**..."

Ephesians 4:6 "...one God and **Father** of all, who is over all and through all and in all."

Ephesians 5:20 "...always giving thanks to God the **Father** for everything, in the name of our Lord Jesus Christ."

Ephesians 6:23 "Peace to the brothers and sisters, and love with faith from God the **Father** and the Lord Jesus Christ."

Philippians 1:2 "Grace and peace to you from God our **Father** and the Lord Jesus Christ."

Philippians 2:11 "...and every tongue acknowledge that Jesus Christ is Lord, to the glory of God the **Father**."

Philippians 4:20 "To our God and **Father** be glory for ever and ever. Amen."

Colossians 1:2-3 "To God's holy people in Colossae, the faithful brothers and sisters in Christ: Grace and peace to you from God our **Father**. We always thank God, the **Father** of our Lord Jesus Christ, when we pray for you..."

Colossians 1:12 "...and giving joyful thanks to the **Father**, who has qualified you to share in the inheritance of his holy people in the kingdom of light."

Colossians 3:17 "And whatever you do, whether in word or deed, do it all in the name of the Lord Jesus, giving thanks to God the **Father** through him."

1 Thessalonians 1:1 "Paul, Silas and Timothy, To the church of the Thessalonians in God the **Father** and the Lord Jesus Christ: Grace and peace to you."

1 Thessalonians 1:3 "We remember before our God and **Father** your work produced by faith, your labor prompted by love, and your endurance inspired by hope in our Lord Jesus Christ."

1 Thessalonians 3:11 "Now may our God and **Father** himself and our Lord Jesus clear the way for us to come to you."

1 Thessalonians 3:13 "May he strengthen your hearts so that you will be blameless and holy in the presence of our God and **Father** when our Lord Jesus comes with all his holy ones."

2 Thessalonians 1:1-2 "Paul, Silas and Timothy, To the church of the Thessalonians in God our **Father** and the Lord Jesus Christ: Grace and peace to you from God the **Father** and the Lord Jesus Christ."

2 Thessalonians 2:16 "May our Lord Jesus Christ himself and God our **Father**, who loved us and by his grace gave us eternal encouragement and good hope..."

1 Timothy 1:2 "To Timothy my true son in the faith: Grace, mercy and peace from God the **Father** and Christ Jesus our Lord."

2 Timothy 1:2 "To Timothy, my dear son: Grace, mercy and peace from God the **Father** and Christ Jesus our Lord."

Titus 1:4 "To Titus, my true son in our common faith: Grace and peace from God the **Father** and Christ Jesus our Savior."

- Hebrews 1:5 "For to which of the angels did God ever say, 'You are my Son; today I have become your **Father**'? Or again, 'I will be his **Father**, and he will be my Son'"?

Hebrews 5:5 "In the same way, Christ did not take on himself the glory of becoming a high priest. But God said to him, 'You are my Son; today I have become your **Father**.'"

Hebrews 12:9 "Moreover, we have all had human fathers who disciplined us and we respected them for it. How much more should we submit to the **Father** of spirits and live!"

James 1:17 "Every good and perfect gift is from above, coming down from the **Father** of the heavenly lights, who does not change like shifting shadows."

James 1:27 "Religion that God our **Father** accepts as pure and faultless is this: to look after orphans and widows in their distress and to keep oneself from being polluted by the world."

James 3:9 "With the tongue we praise our Lord and **Father**, and with it we curse human beings, who have been made in God's likeness."

1 Peter 1:2-3 "...who have been chosen according to the foreknowledge of God the **Father**, through the sanctifying work of the Spirit, to be obedient to Jesus Christ and sprinkled with his blood: Grace and peace be yours in abundance. Praise be to the God and **Father** of our Lord Jesus Christ! In his great

mercy he has given us new birth into a living hope through the resurrection of Jesus Christ from the dead..."

1 Peter 1:17 "Since you call on a **Father** who judges each person's work impartially, live out your time as foreigners here in reverent fear."

2 Peter 1:17 "He received honor and glory from God the **Father** when the voice came to him from the Majestic Glory, saying, 'This is my Son, whom I love; with him I am well pleased.'"

1 John 1:2-3 "The life appeared; we have seen it and testify to it, and we proclaim to you the eternal life, which was with the **Father** and has appeared to us. We proclaim to you what we have seen and heard, so that you also may have fellowship with us. And our fellowship is with the **Father** and with his Son, Jesus Christ."

1 John 2:1 "My dear children, I write this to you so that you will not sin. But if anybody does sin, we have an advocate with the **Father**—Jesus Christ, the Righteous One."

1 John 2:14 "I write to you, dear children, because you know the **Father**. I write to you, fathers, because you know him who is from the beginning. I write to you, young men, because you are strong, and the word of God lives in you, and you have overcome the evil one."

1 John 2:15-16 "Do not love the world or anything in the world. If anyone loves the world, love for the **Father** is not in them. For everything in the world—the lust of the flesh, the lust of the eyes, and the pride of life—comes not from the **Father** but from the world."

1 John 2:22-24 "Who is the liar? It is whoever denies that Jesus is the Christ. Such a person is the antichrist—denying the **Father** and the Son. No one who denies the Son has the **Father**; whoever acknowledges the Son has the **Father** also. As for you, see that what you have heard from the beginning remains in you. If it does, you also will remain in the Son and in the **Father**."

1 John 3:1 "See what great love the **Father** has lavished on us, that we should be called children of God! And that is what we are! The reason the world does not know us is that it did not know him."

1 John 4:14 "And we have seen and testify that the **Father** has sent his Son to be the Savior of the world."

1 John 5: 1 (AMPC) "Everyone who believes (adheres to, trusts, and relies on the fact) that Jesus is the Christ (the Messiah) is a born-again child of God; and everyone who loves the **Father** also loves the one born of Him (His offspring)."

2 John 1:3-4 "Grace, mercy and peace from God the **Father** and from Jesus Christ, the **Father**'s Son, will be with us in truth and love. It has given me great joy to find some of your children walking in the truth, just as the **Father** commanded us."

2 John 1:9 "Anyone who runs ahead and does not continue in the teaching of Christ does not have God; whoever continues in the teaching has both the **Father** and the Son."

Jude 1:1 "Jude, a servant of Jesus Christ and a brother of James, To those who have been called, who are loved in God the **Father** and kept for Jesus Christ..."

Revelation 1:6 "...and has made us to be a kingdom and priests to serve his God and **Father**—to him be glory and power for ever and ever! Amen."

Revelation 2:27 "...that one 'will rule them with an iron scepter and will dash them to pieces like pottery'—just as I have received authority from my **Father**."

Revelation 3:5 "The one who is victorious will, like them, be dressed in white. I will never blot out the name of that person from the book of life, but will acknowledge that name before my **Father** and his angels."

Revelation 3:21 "To the one who is victorious, I will give the right to sit with me on my throne, just as I was victorious and sat down with my **Father** on his throne."

Revelation 14:1 "Then I looked, and there before me was the Lamb, standing on Mount Zion, and with him 144,000 who had his name and his **Father**'s name written on their foreheads."

Prayers of Submission

Daily Prayer of Surrender and Submission

Father God, I humbly surrender and submit myself fully to You and your leadership by Your Holy Spirit.

Lord, please forgive me for both my willful and my unintentional sins. Help me to freely and fully forgive others as You forgive me.

Father, I submit willingly and completely to your Hand as The Potter. Re-make me into the person You want me to be for the plan You have for me in Your perfect will. As You do, conform me to the image of Jesus by the sanctifying work of Your Holy Spirit.

Father, by Your grace help me to always be a grateful, humble heir of all Your promises; an obedient, faithful servant of all Your commands; a persistent, bold witness of Your salvation through Jesus; and, a loving, trusting child full of Your love. I surrender to Your Holy Spirit's leadership.

Let me be patient and persevering in prayer, ever watchful and responsive for opportunities to bless others as You have blessed me. Empower me Father with Your grace, through the Spirit of Jesus in me, to diligently seek You and Your eternal Kingdom, so that I will not be distracted and overcome with the temptations and temporary pleasures of this alien world. In everything I think, say and do today, Father, let me continually glorify and honor You.

I love You, Jesus. I praise You and adore You for first loving me. Thank You for being made sin for me so that I am made righteous in You. Please love and bless others through me today as I seek to know and do Your perfect will for my life. I want to be led today by Your Holy Spirit in me.

In the power of the blood of Jesus, and the authority of His Name I pray. Amen.

Prayer of Submissive Obedience in a Particular Area

Father, You are worthy of all praise, honor, and glory. I adore You. I worship You. I praise Your Holy Name.

Lord, You have been so patient with me, and I thank You. I also recognize Your still, small voice, speaking to me about an area of my life that needs resolution. You have been reminding me of my need to move ahead in this certain area, and I confess that I have not yet obeyed You. Please forgive me for my hesitation.

Today, I declare that I will take the step of faith You have spoken to me about. Lord, in regard to this step that I have been hesitant to take, I put away all my reluctance now, and I pledge to You that I will obey You.

And Lord, in those matters where I have been doing what You would prefer that I not do, I lay them aside, so that I can make room to do what You want me to do.

This is the way I choose to walk with you from now on. Laying aside my hesitancy and stubbornness, I step boldly, choosing You and Your purposes for my life. I declare that I will follow You in obedience.

Thank You, Lord! In Jesus' Name I pray. Amen.

Note: "The Prayer of Submissive Obedience in a Particular Area" was from a teaching by Derek Prince, www.derekprince.org.

Confessions for Every Day

Loved One in Christ-Build your faith and claim God's promises for yourself by reading these confessions of God's Word aloud (thoughtfully and prayerfully - with conviction) every day. Keep doing it until they are your thoughts so that you can use the Word against Satan to "take every thought captive" when he attacks your mind! To "confess" is to say the same thing as God, so that as the Word transforms your mind, His thoughts become your thoughts! Confess these daily at least once - early morning is best so you are "armed and dangerous" when Satan attacks during the day! Before bedtime is good too so you are protected as you rest.

- I am not just an ordinary man/woman. I'm a child of the living God. I am not just a person; I'm an heir of God, and a joint heir with Jesus Christ. I'm not "just an old sinner," I am a new creation in Jesus, my Lord. I'm part of a chosen generation, a Royal Priesthood, a Holy Nation. I'm one of God's people. I am His. I am a living witness of His grace, mercy and love!

- I have been crucified with Christ and I no longer live, but Christ lives in me! The life I live in the body, I live by the faith of the Son of God, who loved me, and gave Himself for me. When the devil tries to resurrect the "old man," I will rebuke him and remind him sternly that I am aware of his tricks, lures, lies and deception. The "old man" is dead. My "new man" knows all old things are passed away-all things have become new!

- I'm not under guilt or condemnation. I refuse discouragement, for it is not of God. God is the God of all encouragement. There is therefore now no condemnation for those in Christ Jesus. Satan is a liar. I will not listen to his accusations.

- I gird up my loins of my mind. I am cleansed in the Blood. No weapon formed against me shall prosper, and I shall condemn every tongue rising against me in judgment. I am accepted in the beloved. If God be for me, who can be against me?

- My mind is being renewed by the Word of God. I pull down strongholds; I cast down imaginations; I bring every thought captive to the obedience of Christ.

- As the Father loves Jesus, so Jesus loves me. I'm the righteousness of God in Christ. I'm not slave of sin; I am a slave of God and a slave of righteousness. I continue in His Word; I know the truth and I practice it, so the truth sets me free.

- Because the Son sets me free, I am free indeed. He who is born of God keeps me, therefore the evil one does not touch me. I've been delivered out of the kingdom of darkness. I am now part of the Kingdom of Light, the Kingdom of God. I don't serve sin any longer. Sin has no dominion over me.

- I will not believe the enemy's lies. He will not intimidate me. He is a liar and the father of lies. Satan is defeated. For this purpose, the Son of God came into this world – to destroy the works of the devil. No longer will he oppress me. Surely, oppression makes a wise person mad. I will get mad at the devil. I defeat him by the Blood of the Lamb, by the word of my testimony as to what He has done for me, not loving my life, even to death.

- I will submit to God. I will resist the devil and he will flee. No temptation will overtake me that is not common to man. God is Faithful and True; He will not let me be tempted beyond my strength, but with the temptation He will also provide the way of escape (Jesus) that I may be able to endure.

- I will stand fast in the liberty with which Christ has made me free. Where the Spirit of the Lord is, there is liberty – not liberty to do what I "want," but freedom to do as I "ought." The law of the Spirit of Life in Christ Jesus has set me free from the law of sin and death.

- Nothing can separate me from the love of God that is in Christ Jesus, my Lord. His Holy Spirit is my guide, comforter, teacher and best friend! Jesus is my Protector, my Deliverer, my Rewarder, my Refuge, my Strong Tower, my Shepherd, my Light, my Life, my Counselor, my Rock, my Freedom! He is everything to me!

- Christ causes me to triumph. I will reign as a king in life through Christ Jesus. As a young man/woman I am strong. The Word of God abides in me, and I have overcome the evil one. I am more than a conqueror through Christ who loves me. I am an overcomer. I am invincible. I can do all things through Christ who strengthens me. Thanks be to God who gives me the victory through Jesus Christ, my Lord!

WISDOM AND GUIDANCE CONFESSIONS

- The Spirit of Truth abides in me and teaches me all things, and He guides me into all truths. Therefore, I confess I have perfect knowledge of every situation and circumstance I come up against, for I have the wisdom of God. (John 16:13; James 1:5)

- I trust in the Lord with all my heart and I do not lean or rely on my own understanding. In all my ways I acknowledge Him, and He directs my path. (Proverbs 3:5-6)

- The Lord will perfect that which concerns me, and fulfill His purpose for me. (Psalm 138:8)

- I let the Word of Christ dwell in me richly in all wisdom. (Colossians 3:16)

- I do follow the Good Shepherd, and I know His voice. The voice of a stranger I will not follow. (John 10:4-5)

- Jesus is made unto me wisdom, righteousness, sanctification, and redemption. Therefore, I confess I have the wisdom of God, and I am the righteousness of God in Christ Jesus. (I Cor. 1:30; II Cor. 5:21)

- I am filled with the knowledge of the Lord's will in all wisdom and spiritual understanding. (Colossians 1:9)

- I am a new creation in Christ. I am His workmanship created in Christ Jesus. Therefore, I have the mind of Christ and the wisdom of God is formed within me. (II Cor. 5:17; Ephesians 2:10; I Cor. 2:16)

- I receive the Spirit of wisdom and revelation in the knowledge of Him, the eyes of my understanding being enlightened. I am not conformed to this world but I am transformed by the renewing of my mind. My mind is renewed by the Word of God. (Ephesians 1:17-18; Romans 12:2)

I AM...

- I am forgiven. (Col. 1:13-14)
- I am saved by grace through faith. (Eph. 2:8)
- I am delivered from the powers of darkness. (Col. 1:13)
- I am led by the Spirit of God. (Rom. 8:14)
- I am kept in safety wherever I go. (Psalm 91:11-12)
- I am getting all my needs met by Jesus. (Phil. 4:19)
- I am casting all my cares on Jesus. (1 Peter 5:7)
- I am not anxious or worried about anything. (Phil. 4:6)
- I am strong in the Lord and in the power of His might. (Eph. 6:10)
- I am doing all things through Christ who strengthens me. (Phil. 4:13)
- I am observing and doing the Lord's commandments. (Deut. 28:13)
- I am blessed going in and blessed going out. (Deut. 28:6)

- I am above only and not beneath. (Deut. 28:13)
- I am blessed with all spiritual blessings. (Eph. 1:3)
- I am healed by His stripes. (I Peter 2:24)
- I am more than a conqueror. (Romans 8:37)
- I am an overcomer by the Blood of the Lamb and the word of my testimony. (Rev. 12:11)
- I am not moved by what I see. (II Cor. 4:8-9)
- I am walking by faith and not by sight. (II Cor. 5:7)
- I am daily overcoming the Devil. (I John 4:4)
- I am casting down vain imaginations. (II Cor. 10:4)
- I am bringing every thought into captivity. (II Cor.10:5)
- I am not conformed to this world, but I am being transformed by renewing my mind. (Romans 12:1-2)
- I am blessing the Lord at all times and continually praising the Lord with my mouth. (Psalm 34:1)
- I am a child of God. (Romans 8:16)

Personalized Daily Prayers

LOVED ONE IN CHRIST:

These passages of scripture from Paul, David, and Isaiah have been personalized for you. They are powerful prayers, by powerful men, to the Most Powerful! As you pray God's Word back to Him, He is pleased, for He has told us to put Him in remembrance of His Word. Do you think He needs to be reminded? Like He forgot? No, we are the ones who need to be reminded. We claim these awesome promises for ourselves. Pray these daily as the Spirit leads you. You will be richly blessed in doing so.

IN THE NAME OF JESUS,

I praise you Lord from my soul. From my inmost being I praise your Holy Name. I praise you Lord from my soul. I will not forget all your benefits – you forgive all my sins and heal all my diseases. You redeemed my life from the pit and crowned me with your love and compassion. You satisfy my desires with good things so that my youth is renewed like an eagle's. Amen. (Psalm 103:1-5)

IN THE NAME OF JESUS,

As I dwell in the shelter of the Most High I will rest in the shadow of the Almighty. I will say of you Lord, "You are my refuge and my fortress. You are my God and I will trust in you." Surely you will save me from the fowler's snare and from the deadly pestilence. You will cover me with your feathers, and under your wings I will find refuge; your faithfulness will be my shield and rampart.

I will not fear the terror of night nor the arrow that flies by day, nor the pestilence that stalks in the darkness, nor the plague that destroys at midday. A thousand may fall at my side, ten thousand by my right hand, but it will not come near me.

I will observe with my eyes and see the punishment of the wicked. I will make the Most High my dwelling – the Lord is my refuge – so that no harm will befall me, no disaster will come near my tent. God, you will command your angels concerning me to guard me in all my ways; they will lift me up in their hands, so that I will not strike my foot against a stone. I will tread upon the lion and the cobra; I will trample the great lion and the serpent.

Lord, you said because I love you, you will rescue me. You will protect me, for I acknowledge your name. I will call upon you and you will answer me; you will be with me in trouble, you will deliver me and honor me. With long life will you satisfy me and show me your salvation. Amen. (Psalm 91)

IN THE NAME OF JESUS,

No weapon forged against me will prevail and I will refute every tongue that accuses me. This is my heritage as a servant of the Lord, and this is my vindication from you. Amen. (Isaiah 54:17)

IN THE NAME OF JESUS,

I keep asking that you, God of my Lord Jesus Christ, my glorious Father, may give me the Spirit of wisdom and revelation that I may know you better. I pray also that the eyes of my heart may be enlightened in order that I may know the hope to which you have called me, the riches of your glorious inheritance in the saints, and your incomparably great power for us who believe. That power is like the working of your mighty strength, which you exerted in Christ when you raised Him from the dead and seated Him at your right hand in heavenly realms, far above all rule and authority, power and dominion, and every title that can be given, not only in the present age but also in the one to come. And you, God, placed all things under His feet and appointed Him to be over everything for the church, which is His body, the fullness of Him who fills everything in every way. Amen. (Ephesians 1:17-23)

IN THE NAME OF JESUS,

I pray that out of your glorious riches you may strengthen me with power through your Spirit in my inner being, so that Christ may dwell in my heart through faith. And I pray that as I am rooted and established in love, I may have power, together with all the saints, to grasp how wide and long and high and deep is the love of Christ, and that I may know this love that surpasses knowledge – that I may be filled to the measure of all your fullness.

Now to you, God, who is able to do immeasurably more than all I ask or imagine, according to your power that is at work within me, to you be glory in the church and in Christ Jesus throughout all generations, forever and ever! Amen. (Ephesians 3:16-21)

IN THE NAME OF JESUS,

This also is my prayer: that my love may abound more and more in knowledge and depth of insight, so that I may be able to discern what is best and may be pure and blameless until the day of Christ, filled with the fruit of righteousness that comes through Jesus Christ – to the glory and praise of you, God. Amen. (Philippians 1:9-11)

IN THE NAME OF JESUS,

I pray that you fill me with the knowledge of your will through all spiritual wisdom and understanding. I pray this in order that I may live a life worthy of the Lord Jesus and please Him in every way: bearing fruit in every good work, growing in the knowledge of you, God, so that I may be strengthened with all power according to your glorious might so that I may have great endurance and patience and joyfully give you thanks. Amen. (Colossians 1:9b-11)

Spiraling Down to Depravity

By Stephen Canup

Outwardly, in the world's eyes, I was at the top of the ladder of success, the pinnacle of prosperity, and living the dream. With an office on Park Avenue in New York City, and making nearly $250,000 a year in 1985, I had it made. However, deep inside I had begun to delve into an entirely different life which would later lead to the very depths of depravity, perversion and reprobation.

Part of my destruction was revealed in my previously published personal testimony contained in my first book, *Jail-House Religion: From Park Avenue... to Park Bench... to Prison.*

Today, I am able to fill in some of the sordid details for the purpose of bringing more glory to God believing that more personal transparency will bring increased hope and freedom to others if they too turn their lives totally over to Jesus Christ as Lord and Savior. If God can change me, and He has, He can change anybody!

Having risen close to the very top of the business world as a Certified Public Accountant with the world's largest accounting firm, I maintained an outward persona necessary to achieve and quickly climb the corporate ladder. However, my darkest inner secrets of twisted thinking and behavior were well hidden for a time, and I deceived my very own self–destroying my career, my family and my morals by descending into an ever deepening pit of darkness.

Although I was raised in a Christian home, I was exposed to pornography through childhood friends around age 10. Earlier, at age 6 or so, an older boy was in the woods with me behind my house, and in the process of committing sodomy with me, when my mother's voice rang out from the back door that supper was ready, interrupting him and saving me from his designs.

Both of these events introduced darkness in my soul at a young age giving the enemy a foothold he would use on and off for nearly fifty years to lead me into a secret life beginning with lustful imagination and self-gratification, eventually immersing me in triple XXX theatres and bookstores, and sexual immorality of every kind.

Since being saved in prison at age 57, I praise God that He has delivered me from darkness and from deep bondage to a prior lifestyle of sin, depravity and sexual perversion. Among the many addictions I once had, it was pornography, drugs and alcohol that fueled an immoral lifestyle. This was heightened by the fact that I never consistently took the psych meds prescribed for the bipolar diagnosis I received in 1989 at age 37.

It was as if there was a big, black pit in my soul that constantly demanded chemical and sexual indulgences; but it was never filled or satisfied in spite of everything I tried. Over the twenty years between Park Avenue and Prison, I was empty, bored, searching, seeking and restless. I felt powerless to resist almost every enticement presented me. Although I was once very ashamed of the behaviors to which I was led, I am forever grateful to Jesus Christ for finding me and setting me forever free (see Romans 6:16-23).

Where did it all lead? Without details, here are some of the things I struggled with or participated in over the years before I was saved: bisexual encounters, gender confusion, illicit hook-ups with strangers of both sexes, activities in back rooms of adult bookstores, gay bars, indecent exposure, and compulsive self-gratification. The shame and guilt I felt as a result of this lifestyle contributed to constant hopelessness, depression and several suicide attempts.

Jesus took all my shame so that I could have His righteousness; He took all my rejection upon Himself at Calvary so that I could have His acceptance by the Father. The saving work of Jesus, the love of the Father, and the power of the Holy Spirit are the only things that filled that deep pit inside me. The peace, joy, wholeness and abundance I have in place of the emptiness is impossible to adequately describe; and, I am humbly grateful daily that I am now forever free of the condemnation, torment, guilt, embarrassment, shame, perversion and depravity that dominated my soul and life before I was born again. I am a totally new man in Christ Jesus (2 Corinthians 5:17-21). Praise God!!!

I will say it again, if God can save, deliver, heal and change me; He can save, deliver, heal and change anyone! I have learned to take the wrong kind of thoughts captive quickly so that I do not give in to the almost daily temptations the devil brings (2 Corinthians 10:4-5).

But before I was saved, I fell a mighty long way. I was unemployed for seven years, and homeless for three years, leading up to being sent to prison for the first (and last) time at age 56. My crime was solicitation of a minor and I thought my life would be forever ruined because of the label I now carried of "sex offender." I was sent to a medium security, medium term facility managed by CCA (now CoreCivic) in Nashville, TN, to serve my time.

At Davidson County Jail, before I was sent to prison, I requested something to read and the Chaplain sent me a pocket-size Gideon's New Testament. Reading was something I did often to "escape" when I was homeless, helpless and hopeless. Until I finally was able to go to the prison library, the Bible was the only thing I had to read. Since I had already heard men being made fun of for reading their Bible or going to chapel classes or services, I read mine out of the way of others while on my bunk, both in jail, and later in prison.

For the first ten or twelve months in prison, I stayed pretty much to myself and experienced a lot of fairly severe depression. I was not given any meds for bipolar illness so I was essentially stuck in the manic-depressive phase. No one knew where I was so I had no money on my books and did not receive any visits or letters. Sometimes I got out of my depression and despair enough to play some cards or dominos or watch television., but most of the time I was a loner. I kept reading my Bible a little late at night and in the early morning, but I primarily read spy novels, murder mysteries, and westerns. I did not attend chapel. My time drug by.

As I read my Bible more, I remembered what I had learned in the Baptist church growing up about Jesus forgiving all my sins and that He has a plan for everyone's lives. I had a very hard time believing that still applied to me based on all I had done and how far I had fallen, but I could sense a small glimmer of hope. Could God really accept me, forgive me, and love me? The Bible made it clear that He could and does!

Certainly I blamed myself for where I ended up and for the charges I had. I hated myself and could not bear to look into the mirror when shaving or brushing my teeth. I was overcome with guilt, shame, regret and embarrassment. I began to understand that God forgave me, but I couldn't forgive myself. I thought my past was so bad that I had no future.

In my addictions and sin, I had pushed away every family member and friend. My family didn't even know where I was nor if I was even alive. I had not tried to contact them in five or six years. The fact that I had always been so prideful made it impossible for me to reach out to them while I was homeless and unemployed. Now I was in prison where none of my family had ever been.

A major breakthrough began in February, 2009, when I felt God encouraging me to reach out to and ask forgiveness from my family. Humbling myself enough to write that first letter was so very hard, but I felt a huge burden begin to lift as soon as I mailed it. In a short time, I heard from my two older brothers. They said they weren't holding anything against me and both wanted to know what they could do to help me. Wow, what a miracle!

Then the Lord impressed in my spirit that if my family could forgive me, and He could forgive me, then I needed to forgive myself. Oh my goodness, what a sense of freedom from bondage began to grow in me as I decided to put my past in the past, forgive myself, and trust God with my future one day at a time. I reveal much more about this part of my "awakening" in my longer testimony book, *Jail-House Religion: From Park Avenue... to Park Bench... to Prison.*

I began to have more of a hunger for the Word and much less desire for the all the other books I was using to avoid dealing with my feelings and situation. On my 57th birthday, April 20, 2009, I attended my first Chaplaincy class that would last three months. I declare this date as my official "re-birth" date! Being "born again" is the very best thing that has ever happened to me. If it took going to prison to get my attention, so be it.

Soon after, I started going to Chapel when they called out for "church." People were surprised and made fun of me but I didn't care. I was being progressively filled with hope little by little. Having been absolutely hopeless for years of suicidal depression, this was a very welcome feeling. Then I learned from Jeremiah 29:11-14 that God really did have a plan and a future for me. Yes, even me, a sex offender!

I went "all in" for Jesus. I have never looked back and I have never regretted my commitment, not even for a minute. I began to do every Bible Correspondence course I could get my hands on. I started a Bible study and prayer group in my housing area. For me, "Jail-house Religion" was "the real thing."

My two brothers committed to help me get back to Texas as soon as I discharged my sentence. One of them knew the founder of Freedom in Jesus Prison Ministries, Don Castleberry, who began to correspond with me prior to release. Because I felt God had a call on my life for prison ministry, I moved to Levelland, TX, where Don lived and started volunteering in his ministry. He then agreed to mentor me and we were accountability partners. We spent a lot of quality time together and we have become best friends. I am now President of Freedom in Jesus Prison Ministries., after having been Executive Director for about four years.

After a year under Don Castleberry's supervision, in 2012 I asked him to ordain and license me into the Gospel ministry. In prison, I made the commitment to serve God with all of my heart for all of my days. So on February 23, 2012, in front of fifty or so friends and family members, I publically submitted myself to a higher standard of lifetime accountability to God and the Body of Christ as an ordained minister and a licensed teacher of the Word.

My purpose and passion is to share the love and hope of the Gospel of Jesus Christ with every prisoner and inmate I can.

I will say it again, if God can change me (and He surely has), He can change anyone who will surrender their lives, seek Him with all their heart, and be willing to follow hard after Jesus!

The "Old Man"

Six Months Before Prison (2007)

Stephen Canup

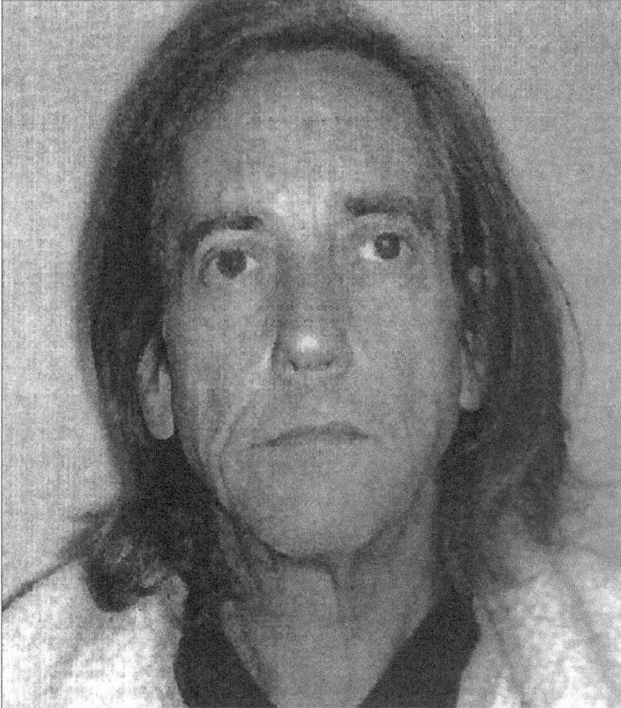

Guilty and Condemned by Sin to Death

Romans 6:23 "For the wages of sin is death...

GUILTY OF THESE SINS AGAINST GOD, OTHERS AND SELF:

Addictions to drugs, alcohol, sex, pornography, praise of men, work

Pride	Judgment	Thievery
Worry	Self-hate	Adultery
Fear	Resentment	Sexual identity
Depression	Regret	Confusion
Hopelessness	Anger	Lying
Anxiety	Covetousness	Conceit
Profanity	Depravity	Intellectualism
Fornication	Reprobation	Humanism
Lustful desires	Un-forgiveness	Shame
Perversion	Immorality	Remorse
Idolatry	Self-abuse	Guilt
Selfishness	Bitterness	Offense

THE SINFUL AND CURSED LIFE I WAS LIVING BEFORE PRISON RESULTED IN ME BEING:

- Homeless, living on the streets of Nashville, TN, for 3 years prior to prison.
- Unemployed for 7 years prior to incarceration.
- Broke after having filed for bankruptcy twice.
- Destitute with all my earthly possessions contained in 1 hanging garment bag in the prison's property room awaiting the day of my release.
- Desolate having abandoned all family and friends, leaving me lonely and utterly forsaken.
- Depressed so deeply by these life conditions that I had attempted suicide several times.
- Hopeless and absolutely convinced nothing would ever change or get better in any way.

The "New Man"

One Year After Prison (2012)

Stephen Canup

A Free Man – Alive in Christ

...but the gift of God is eternal life in Christ Jesus our Lord." Romans 6:23

"I have been crucified with Christ and I no longer live, but Christ lives in me. The life I now live in the body, I live by faith in the Son of God, who loved me and gave himself for me." (Gal. 2:20)

"Therefore if any is (ingrafted) in Christ, the Messiah,
he is (a new creature altogether), a new creation;
the old (previous moral and spiritual condition)
has passed away. Behold, the fresh and new has come!"
(II Cor. 5:17, AMP)

"So if the Son sets you free, you will be free indeed"
(John 8:36)

The new life in Christ that began in prison in 2009 has brought many blessings. As of early 2024, some of these abundant life realities include:

- My spiritual re-birth April 20, 2009!!!
- Restored relationships with every family member.
- A mentor and accountability partner, Don Castleberry, who speaks the truth in love.
- Acceptance instead of rejection.
- Joy and hope instead of depression and hopelessness.
- Purpose and passion to help set others free.
- Peace, boldness and confidence instead of anxiety and fear.
- The righteousness of Christ Jesus instead of perversion and depravity.
- Love and compassion for others instead of selfishness and self-hate.
- Freedom from addictions to alcohol, drugs, pornography, smoking and gambling.
- A tongue of blessings and respect instead of pride, criticism and profanity.
- A beautiful, three bedroom, two bath home provided rent-free except for utilities.

- Three late-model vehicles have been provided to me free, in great condition, with low mileage.
- A house full of good furniture, and a closet full of good clothes.
- Debt-free, with also some money in savings.
- A renewed mind free of all the bad effects of addictions and depression.
- Good health.
- Mature Christians I can call for prayer or advice anytime about anything.
- Licensed and ordained in 2012 as a minister of the Gospel of Jesus Christ.
- President of Freedom in Jesus Prison Ministries.
- Author of six books to encourage the body of Christ behind razor wire.

NOTES

NOTES

STEPHEN CANUP

AND

FREEDOM IN JESUS PRISON MINISTRIES

HEARTILY RECOMMENDS

KINGDOM TOWERS

LUBBOCK, TX

AS A GREAT PLACE TO START OVER!

🌐 Prison Alliance

Write us a letter and enroll
in our Bible Study today!
PO Box 97095, Raleigh, NC 27624